GARY LIBRARY
VERMONT COLLEGE
36 COLLEGE STREET
MONTPELIER, VT 05602
WITHDRAWN
P9-BAW-176

Please remember that this is a library book, and that it belongs only temporarily to each person who uses it. Be considerate. Do not write in this, or any, library book.

WORLD UNDERWORLD

By the same author
LIMPY

Andrew Varna

WORLD UNDERWORLD

LONDON
MUSEUM PRESS LIMITED

First published in Great Britain in 1957 *by*
Museum Press Limited, 26 *Old Brompton Road, London, S.W.*7

364
V317w
1957

Printed in Great Britain by
BARNICOTTS LIMITED
at THE WESSEX PRESS
TAUNTON, SOMERSET

CONTENTS

Chapter *Page*

1. What *is* the Underworld? 7
2. Confidence Men and Women . . . 16
3. Pickpockets 35
4. "The Mafia" 57
5. Interpol 70
6. Prostitution 82
7. Bank-Robbers and Safe-Breakers . . . 104
8. Cardsharps and Gamblers 120
9. Dope and Smuggling 136
10. Counterfeiters and Forgers 158
11. Thieves and Receivers 178

I

what *is* the underworld?

THE Underworld. Every modern man and woman who can read knows of this dark continent of crime that reaches out all over the globe. The newspapers talk of it all the time. Their readers never fail to be attracted by the tale of violence, dishonesty and lust which seethes about them continually and is brought to light as news. Normal, law-abiding people are horrified, fascinated, revolted, appalled, shocked—and always interested in the tales of evil men who are said to control great empires of crime and vice.

Whether it is local crime, city rackets or international vice, the average man likes to read about it. Why? Is it because he likes to have a constant warning in front of him, a perpetual reminder of the folly of sin? Is it because he feels that the more he knows about wickedness the less likely it is to touch him and his family? Or is it because, being honest and leading an unexciting life of drab routine, he secretly admires the lawless ones, the rebels against discipline and convention and rules and regulations?

What is the underworld, this great community of outcasts? How is it controlled, or rather, exploited, by the big bosses of crime? Is there such a thing as an organized network of crime, directed by master-minds and operated with ruthless and savage cunning to enable the lawless ones to live like princes without ever giving anything to the normal world in return?

Here, for the first time, is an attempt to provide the average man and woman with an authoritative survey of world crime. It is presented without any of the glamorous trappings of big, black headlines, stripped of all its glitter and false pretence, and discussed calmly and thoroughly. This is the sanest way to review the underworld and the criminals who populate it.

After all, law-breakers—even the most brutal of them—are basically the same as the rest of us. But there is also a basic difference. They are prepared to risk anything for the sake of living without working, and, in achieving this mental attitude to life, they have also managed to stifle all the impulses of honesty and fair-play which make civilized life possible for the majority. Why do these people refuse to accept the rules, why do they refuse to operate within the law?

This is not a pleasant story, this review of crime throughout the world. Nor is it meant to be. But it is not written with the intention of pointing a moral, or of advising other people how to go about their business in fighting the lawbreakers. The task of apprehending criminals is one for the police, the punishment of wrongdoers is the duty of the courts. The ethics and morals of modern society are the responsibility of the church, the government and the individual.

But these facts will not prevent us from drawing certain conclusions, or disclosing certain obvious fallacies and injustices as we proceed along our dark journey. We will paint black as black and never as any shade of grey.

The world has never been without crime, but organized crime, always a reflection of the society and the conditions in which it flourishes, has never been so powerful. In the fast-moving, closely-linked international society of crooks that to-day can travel the world and exploit the highly intricate and involved organization of big city life, organized crime has reached a peak of wealth and efficiency never before known.

Currency, gold, drugs, jewels, political corruption—these are the articles in the contemporary merchandise of evil. The rewards are vast, and the uneasy climate of international tensions, outbreaks of violence and threats of wholesale annihilation—all these factors make for the growing development of crime.

Man's conquest of distance by communication systems and aviation has made the world a small place in some ways, but for the modern master-criminal it has enlarged the possibilities beyond all imagining. Crime flourishes in wartime like flowers in the desert after rain, for, as soon as some of the barriers of civilized living are down, as soon as violence and mass movement of peoples becomes the normal background to life, then the crooks can operate with immensely greater ease and vastly greater chances of success. Even when peace is restored it takes a long time for supplies to become normal again, and wherever there are shortages of necessities or luxuries, there the criminals thrive and prosper. For the crooks of the world there is no alternative choice between guns or butter—either commodity will do to make a dishonest living.

There is a mystery in all this. How is it that criminals do so well? Why is it that our organized systems of law and order and punishment cannot curb lawlessness more effectively? The underworld could be cut down to size in a year or so if only police methods worked efficiently, and the courts were ruthless in their allotment of punishment. Crime would continue, of course, because wherever there is human behaviour there is good and evil. But the prosperity, the arrogance and the power of the men who live outside the law, could be crushed. It could be crushed if the law operated against the big shots of crime as effectively as it does against John Citizen when he is caught without a radio licence, or when he parks his car in a prohibited area.

By striking hard, and without exception, at the big criminals the running sore of the underworld could be cauterized, and the wound healed cleanly. If police all over the world were beyond corruption, if political influence could not be swayed by the insidious persuasion of graft (and these are mighty big "ifs") then the world could be rid of the curse of organized crime.

This book deals with the many major aspects of crime. It is not written by a policeman, by a lawyer or a social welfare worker. It is written by a man who has been in the vast network of international crime—a man who has been a member of the shadowy, half-world that exists and thrives outside the law. Because of this, it tells a story of the people who seem so remote from the reality of honest living—the long round of work and thrift and more work—from the inside, and without any exclamations of horror and disgust. Criminals, in short, are people. They grow old, have toothache, are as frightened of age and death as any normal citizen, and, many of them, yearn for security and a quiet life as the passing years slow down their youthful fire.

They are not, of course, likely to achieve the peace and security they desire. They have flouted the law for too long, or too violently, for society's forces of law and order to let them alone. And the result is, they must keep moving, keep striving for the big coup that will buy them a few years of peace in hiding. It is an expensive business, this bid for freedom outside the law, and every man in the jungle of underworld is vulnerable to any other crook who seeks to make money from his guilty life. If they are robbed, these criminal veterans, they cannot complain. They suffer their losses in silence—and plan their revenge on the society of decent citizens whose ranks they can never enter.

Crime pays, all right, but not the same dividends as honest endeavour. The profits of crime are the gaudy prizes of high living, glittering cold-eyed women, sleek cars, and a sort of power that is based on the ready bank-roll and terror. But there is no security, no easing up from the perpetual struggle to survive by toughness, and very little of the solid loyalty and love of friends and family that bring life's reward to "the mugs" who work for a living and grow old and die without ever knowing the thrill of success the easy way.

This book deals with the major aspects of organized crime, the big rackets, and the highly developed professions of lawless prosperity. It includes chapters on safe-breakers and bank robbers (the "engineers" of crime who plan their raids as shrewdly as a financier making a big killing on the stock market), burglars (the humble tradesmen of the underworld), forgers and counterfeiters, the Mafia (the world-wide network of Sicilian criminals, thugs and parasites, with members involved in every racket that exists), white slavers and prostitution (the sordid accompaniment of crime that provides the nearest approach to "love" some criminals ever know), pickpockets (the skilled trade of the lawless world), confidence tricksters (the "artists" of crime), extortion racketeers, dope smugglers (the underworld's men without conscience), cardsharps and gamblers, and—to provide an insight into the forces that wage ceaseless war on the outcast society that lives on mankind, but never with it—a section on *Interpol*, the International Criminal Police Commission.

This book will not attempt a formal history of the various branches of crime, or set out to detail operations of the various criminal syndicates and brotherhoods of violence and vice. But it will outline the facts of underworld life, give examples of the way honest men can be tricked, because almost every man alive likes to get something for nothing, and trace the general, loose pattern of co-operation between criminals of all races and creeds in their campaign to survive outside the law.

The term "underworld" embraces every aspect of illegal activity, but its origin is obscure. The criminal is always anxious to hide and, in the modern world, strives to build up a front of legality and respectability unless he is no more than a gunman or a coarse thief—the Underworld's "peasants". In the days of the Egyptian tomb robbers the thieves hid in ruins. In the Middle Ages, in Rome and Paris, criminals did retreat "beneath the world" in catacombs, sewers, and in cellars.

But now, the criminal hides under an appearance of normal behaviour. He establishes offices to deal in real estate and peddles drugs; he dresses well and lives at a good address to cover his traffic in stolen diamonds; he aids charities, has a good bank reference and a charming outward manner to establish confidence among his wealthy victims. Only the petty criminals hide themselves during the day and come out on the prowl at night.

What makes the Underworld so dangerous and such a drain on the economy of the modern state is its members' belief that they must make an easy living. The fact that they risk arrest, imprisonment, and even death to get money without working for it, involves them in a much more hazardous and arduous existence than the average lawful citizen ever even imagines. But the criminal pays no taxes, collects his tribute and moves on to fresh victims, with the illusion that he is as carefree as a butterfly sipping honey. These things—the element of risk, of living dangerously and defiantly—develop in him a sense of power. They often create a feeling of superiority, even of privilege.

There is no lack of recruits to the Underworld. Since the war, particularly, large numbers of young men have turned to a life of crime. Many young soldiers returned to find civilian opportunities had passed them by while they were away and they had acquired a lot of new skills in their military life which equipped them ideally for some branches of underworld enterprise. Safe-breakers have been recruited in hundreds in this way. Men got used to handling explosives and developed a high technical knowledge of their use in the army. Many ex-soldiers also became accustomed to an easy life in the armed forces and felt no inclination to settle down to hard work once they were demobilized. A life of occasional risks interspersed with long periods of inactivity is just what the Underworld offers, and it is remarkably like the tempo of life in the services. Soldiering can, and does in many instances, fit a man ideally for a life of crime.

The flow of professional experts into the world of crime also increased sharply after the two world wars. Experts in many fields came from Russia, Hungary, Austria, Poland, Czechoslovakia and Rumania, having survived, many of them, long embittering years in concentration camps. Their normal lives were in ruins and it was a perfect opportunity for the established underworld operators to gather them in. They brought with them, of course, many new ideas, and the Underworld is always hungry for new ideas.

Modern penalties for crime, it should be remembered, are nothing like the harsh and inhuman punishments meted out to wrongdoers in ancient days, when a thief might lose his hands, a swindler have his tongue torn out, or his eyes removed. There were other penalties, such as being sent to the galleys or to salt mines, which amounted to death. Only in the past hundred years have some of these barbaric cruelties been abandoned. To-day's criminal risks only imprisonment.

Even this fate may be avoided or eased by skilful legal representation and shrewd appeals to have sentences reduced. A strong argument against cruel punishments could be made out from the criminal statistics of the nineteenth century, when even the British threat of transportation to Australia and other penal colonies did nothing to deter violent crime in those harsh days. And the notorious French penal prison on Devil's Island did not reduce crime in France noticeably. Both systems, however, brutalized its victims and may, possibly, have stepped up the incidence of violent crime by making criminals more desperate in resisting arrest.

But no matter how successful a criminal is, he always is a prey to his fellows, and always a man on the defensive. These bonds of insecurity make it inevitable that they mix only with their own kind, and even then, without any real trust or friendship. This limited existence perfects their knowledge of dishonest and violent survival, polishes their skill into an art in some instances, and produces only one unshakeable standard of behaviour—never tell the cops anything.

Our review of organized crime may appear to show that "underworld" is a loose term that destroys the popular illusion of crime operating as an international network of villainy. But there is an intangible and unwritten code of crime that ensures help and protection for criminals among criminals wherever they may find themselves.

Just as all sorts of incongruous types are united in fighting shoulder to shoulder to defend a nation in time of war, the criminal population is always united, to a degree, in its struggle against the law. The organization is sometimes formal and explicit (as in some of the branches of the Mafia), sometimes it is voluntary and haphazard, but it always exists.

If a criminal, having made his pile, wishes to withdraw from the underworld he may not find this easy. Indeed, he may find it impossible. His fellows know nothing of decency where money is concerned—they have no understanding of, nor sympathy for, the individual's right to live his own life and let the rest of the world go by. If a criminal has money he is as much a victim as any honest man. In fact, he is an easier victim than an honest man, because the criminal dare not seek protection from the police. He has only his own strength and villainy to protect him.

The types of co-operation among crooks, like the lawful associations to promote common interests among honest men, are infinitely varied, both in manner and degree. There are local groups who specialize in one aspect of crime, but are ready to join forces with other crooks in protecting each other from the police or in organizing the distribution of stolen goods. This type of co-operation seldom extends to the planning and execution of major criminal enterprises, but it can overlap in the secondary fields of crime, in covering up and in exchanging information.

The crime bosses of to-day are seldom supreme because of their physical strength. They are either outstandingly callous and efficient gunmen with a flair for inspiring loyalty among a small group of equally ruthless killers, or they have all the virtues that go to shape the captain of industry. They are shrewd, level-headed and forceful personalities, with more brains and determination than the run-of-the-mill thugs whose perverted courage they use as cleverly as any normal employer uses his workers' skill and pride of craft to make profits for the management.

Most American gangs begin as neighbourhood teams of adolescent hoodlums, or as sinister partnerships formed in gaol among established criminals. These people not only learn each other's strengths and weaknesses, but share a common knowledge that binds them together as much for power as for fear of reprisal, should they drift away from the mob.

The ruthless crop of gangsters produced in the feverish 'twenties' in New York and Chicago are now middle-aged—those who have survived. And a middle-aged criminal is either successful and wealthy, or poor and defeated. There are hardly any "average criminals" living out their lives in comparative ease.

There are cases, which will be presented in the course of our survey, of successful gangsters who now lead lives of retirement, pay their taxes and strive to launch their families into the law-abiding world, but they are few. The parasites, the ageing brutalized and embittered crooks whose only chance of existing in even mild comfort is to blackmail their former associates, give the "retired" criminals little rest. They are dependants who cost a lot of money, but never entitle the man who supports them to any relief on his income tax return.

What makes a man, or a woman, a criminal? It is the fashion now to explain the development of a criminal personality by tracing some early experience which warped an otherwise happy life. Poverty, cruelty, injustice, horror—any violent emotional misfortune in youth can be accepted as the origin of a life of crime. There is little that can be done to avoid these misfortunes. In many cases the psychologists can frame a most convincing case on these lines, but there is a factor in the growth of the Underworld which could be changed. It is the provision of schools for criminality, training grounds in vice and brutality which mould the vast majority of lawbreakers into a shape that can never be broken once it is established. These colleges of crime are the prisons and gaols and reformatories.

Gaol is the Crime University of the Underworld. It is in gaol that the newcomer to crime absorbs his lasting hatred for authority, his defiance of law, and his contempt for earning a living in the conventional manner. Early offenders, confined with hardened crooks, learn fast—and they learn all the wrong things.

Many young hoodlums, or delinquents, are youths of more than average intellgence, initiative and courage. Their cunning and physical daring, destined to be used against the law, could just as easily ensure them success and infinitely greater happiness in normal life. But a few months on the side of the lawless and their lives are devoted to crime, with all the passionate conviction only youth can develop.

The case for separate prisons for first offenders, institutions where immensely greater efforts at rehabilitation could be made than at present, is essential if the Underworld is to be defeated. Without recruits, the powerful community of the lawless would soon wither and waste away to become nothing more than an occasional and minor nuisance. The time to be patient with a criminal is early in his career. It is little use devoting thousands of pounds of the taxpayer's money to patiently guarding a criminal's later years in prison, for it is then the younger generation of lawbreakers can mix with the veterans, pick up their attitudes and criminal lore, and go out again as newly graduated enemies of society.

Crime is born anywhere a man prefers to take a risk, rather than work for a living. It grows and thrives wherever human beings are victims of circumstance. It develops into organized evil wherever some individual has the ability to plan and to inspire leadership. It achieves power and the glitter of riches wherever criminals are allowed to work out some system of mutual tolerance with police and politicans.

Its world is a paradox—at once far removed from the average man, and yet rubbing shoulders with him every day of his life. It attracts and repels, fascinates and disgusts the decent citizen with all the power of the unknown. The purpose of this book is to strip the mystery from the Underworld, to present it factually and without emotion.

Only by looking at it carefully and dispassionately can the normal world ever hope to understand it, and by understanding it hope to destroy its widespread evil.

2

confidence men and women

SOME of the greatest actors in the world never set foot on a stage. They perform without greasepaint, without footlights, without applause and without a script. But, although their audience is generally (and preferably) only one, they receive thousands of pounds for a good performance. A bad one, however, lands them in gaol—or in hospital, if their "audience" should prove capable of violence. These great actors are the confidence men, the elite of the Underworld. They are men of considerable charm, fine appearance, superb poise and utter and complete dishonesty.

There have always been tricksters of one sort or another, and there will always be victims for their wiles as long as greed is a human failing. It is greed that enables the confidence man to get away with his act and, from the way the victims are fooled, greed must be next only to love in blinding the normal man or woman's commonsense vision.

The confidence man has for his tools a ready wit, a cool nerve, an ability to play a part to perfection and, of course, plenty of cheek or confidence. That is all.

Judge for yourself the skill with which he uses them. He is sitting at a table in the dining room of the Waldorf-Astoria in New York. He is beautifully dressed in a dark-blue worsted suit, light-grey tie and highly polished shoes, hair neatly groomed and greying a little at the temples. His hands are manicured to perfection. He is talking to a casual acquaintance who has come to New York from the Middle West where he has made a fortune from a chain of grocery stores.

The confidence man has carefully checked on his man—his bank balance, his history and his vices. He knows that this man, stout and tough though he looks, will tremble at the knees with desire if he gets a chance to make some easy money. But it must not appear to be too easy . . . his man is a hard-headed Mid-Westerner who has had to battle for every one of his million dollars. He is not going to be talked into buying a gold brick or any of those crude propositions that sometimes work with simpler citizens.

The confidence man, using the name of Henry Stewart-Steel, talks easily of golf he played recently at Banff National Park in Canada where he spent a fortnight resting from his work as an importer of English tweeds.

They finish eating and begin to sip their coffee when Stewart-Steel hurriedly puts down his cup with a cry of surprise.

"Well! What do you know! There's Hanson B. Clarke, the sharebroker. He must have come down from Montreal. I saw him there two days ago."

"Is that so," says the Mid-Westerner, politely interested.

"One of the biggest wheat speculators in the world," says Stewart-Steel. "I must go over and speak to him a moment. Perhaps you would care to meet him?"

The Mid-Westerner, always ready to respect a big operator, sees no reason why he shouldn't have this experience. He has even come to think that he's heard of this Hanson B. Clarke, the wheat speculator.

As they finish their coffee, Stewart-Steel explains that Clarke, only a couple of weeks ago, made a million-dollar market killing in Montreal, and that his presence here in New York is probably significant.

"I wonder why he's back on this side of the pond so soon?" muses Stewart-Steel. "Well, let's say hello to him anyway. It never does any harm to be known to these people."

Stewart-Steel, with his new friend in tow, threads his way over to Clarke's table. Clarke looks up coldly as Stewart-Steel approaches.

"Aren't you Mr. Clarke? The man my friend Judge Judson was speaking about in Montreal a week or so ago?" says Stewart-Steel confidently.

"My name is not Clarke and I have never been to Montreal," says Clarke abruptly, turning back to his dignified study of the menu.

"But, I'm sure . . . I was sure it was your picture I saw in the papers there. I'm terribly sorry to have mistaken your face for . . ."

"Are you a journalist?" asks Clarke, with the air of a man about to administer a cruel snub.

"No. I'm just a business man, same as my friend here, Mr. Schubakker, of Milwaukee. We thought we should like to pay a little homage to a man whose reputation is world-wide. We . . ."

Clarke's manner softens. "Very well, gentlemen. I *am* Clarke, and I must admit I was in Montreal last week. But I thought it was a very well-guarded secret, and I'm sick and tired of being pestered by newspapermen who seem to think everything I do is their business. You will excuse my unfriendliness."

Stewart-Steel introduces himself, chats about his friend, Judge Judson in Montreal, and wonders if they might not have a chat after luncheon.

Clarke is sorry he cannot manage that, but he will be delighted if Stewart-Steel and Mr. Schubakker will be his guests at dinner that night.

Before they part, Clarke happens to mention again that he has an aversion to the press and its publicity and, as an example of how embarrassing it can be, he produces several clippings from Montreal papers, which include his picture and stories about his big stock-market killing. "This sort of thing is just a nuisance to a man like myself," he adds—and leaves the clippings on the table.

The stage is set, the cast allotted their proper roles, and now the little drama unfolds skilfully and pleasantly, with Stewart-Steel playing the lead, directing the performance, and yet seeming to be no more than a bystander. Clarke, as carefully briefed in his performance as any actor on the boards, is a little condescending in his manner towards both Stewart-Steel and Schubakker, but, as their dinner party draws to a close, he has mellowed considerably. He may be famous, but he is only human, and it is apparent that he is susceptible to flattery.

He suggests that, perhaps Stewart-Steel might care to be in on a little deal he's planning on the New York Exchange, and to make this possible, he gives Stewart-Steel an operator's pass (a faked one, of course) so that he can buy and sell as one of Clarke's accredited agents.

Schubakker does not see Stewart-Steel for a day or so, but he is obviously interested to know how his friend has fared when they do meet again. Stewart-Steel tries not to appear pleased with himself, but he admits that Clarke's kindness has put him in the way of making eighty thousand dollars. Simple enough, when you know that wheat prices are going to fall one day and rise a few points the next, he explains. And Stewart-Steel has made his profit without having to write a cheque. Clarke's patronage took care of all credit formalities.

"As a matter of fact, I am waiting now for the secretary from the Exchange to bring me my gains," says Stewart-Steel to Schubakker. And, a few moments later, a slim young man in a dark suit approaches carrying a leather satchel. He pauses discreetly after introducing himself, but Stewart-Steel says: "I'll fix it up here, Parker. My friend, Mr. Schubakker saw the beginning of this deal—he may as well see the end of it."

The secretary is still a little diffident and suggests he should have a word in private with Stewart-Steel. But the confidence man insists that the business be discussed openly.

"Mr. Stewart-Steel, there is just one detail I must discuss with you before handing over the proceeds of your market transaction. Mr. Clarke left instructions with us that you should provide us with some proof that your financial position was satisfactory. In fact, Mr. Stewart-Steel, my instructions are that, unless you can show us that you could have borne any losses that might have occurred, we are not prepared to conclude the transaction Mr. Clarke made possible for you. I'm sorry, but . . ."

Stewart-Steel cuts the young man's discomfiture short with a fatherly smile. "Here is the name and telephone number of my bank. You can telephone them, my boy. Call them now, if you wish, and check my standing there. Here," he dives into his pocket, "is my current account balance . . ."

The secretary glances at the proffered cheque book, but takes the telephone number and explains that he must ring the bank. As he goes off, Stewart-Steel laughs a little ruefully and says: "These big men certainly take no chances. But I suppose they must be very careful not to have their names abused. Luckily, I have nothing to worry about."

Schubakker is, however, incensed at the treatment Stewart-Steel has had to endure. "That's a hell of a way to stand a man up, Steel. Why couldn't they have checked on your position before?"

"They haven't had a chance to do any thing, except accept my orders to buy and sell," says Stewart-Steel, quite unruffled. "I expected them to make a check of some kind. These big men move fast when they make a decision. They leave someone else to tidy up on the detail. I felt quite sorry for that young fellow's predicament, really."

Then the secretary hurries back towards them. "Everything is in order, Mr. Stewart-Steel. I'm sorry to have worried you like this, but I'm sure you understand my position."

"Perfectly," says Stewart-Steel, accepting the cash and signing the young man's receipt. (He insisted on cash so that he could more easily avoid taxation.) "Would you care for a drink before you go back?"

"Oh no, thank you, Sir. It is not permitted." The secretary is most deferential, and hurries away.

"After all," says Stewart-Steel, to soothe the still ruffled Schubakker, "one mustn't complain at that small inconvenience for the sake of eighty thousand dollars. Come and be my guest to lunch."

A day or so passes with Stewart-Steel very gradually cementing his new friendship with Schubakker. They go to a show together, dine once or twice, and play a little bridge in the evenings, before Stewart-Steel takes his friend aside one morning and asks him if he would like to be partner in a deal that will turn seventy-five thousand dollars from each man into a profit of three hundred thousand dollars each. It might be a pleasant way of covering his holiday expenses, says Stewart-Steel to Schubakker, and he knows from the glint in Schubakker's eyes that his man is well and truly hooked.

There is, of course, one small matter to be adjusted first. Schubakker must naturally deposit his seventy-five thousand dollars with the brokerage firm, just as a token of good faith and financial standing. The secretary is called back to the hotel again and he tucks Schubakker's cheque into his satchel most apologetically as he goes off with orders to buy, from the two men. To-morrow the deal will be over and Stewart-Steel it is, this time, who is Schubakker's guest to dinner.

To-morrow? Poor Schubakker finds Mr. Stewart-Steel

checked out of the hotel late at night, leaving no forwarding address. How could such a hard-headed business man give a stranger 75 thousand dollars without security? But Schubakker thought he had every security. He had sized Stewart-Steel up himself. He had every reason to trust him and be grateful to him for a chance to make a quick fortune. The whole deal was one of those lucky occasions that come the way of smart business men who know the right people.

Stewart-Steel and Clarke divided their spoils equally. Confidence and greed had been combined once again. The old and trusted recipe had not failed.

The Stewart-Steels of the confidence game are the stars. Their success story reaches across the capital cities of the world, its little dramas set in nothing but the most sumptuous surroundings, and its thefts conducted with the greatest charm. There are lower levels of this performance, of course. There are the diamond traders, the dealers in old paintings, the Persian carpet salesmen, and the men who have remarkable inventions.

The bogus diamond dealers may be nothing but sharp traders who appear to sell fine stones, but they have fake wares to sell. One of the most popular tricks in this litte backwater of the Underworld is the blue-white diamond proposition. Ordinary yellow diamonds, valued at about £60 a carat, can be made to turn into blue-white stones worth five or six times the value, by simply stewing them in boiling water for a few minutes and adding the ground lead from a copying pencil. They are also set in platinum to make them look specially attractive. A child could do the colour-changing, but it takes a master crook to make money from this simple recipe.

Even reputable dealers and pawnshops are caught by this fraud when the sales-talk that goes with it is good enough. But a test as simple as the recipe will expose the fake in a few moments. Just drop a blue-white diamond in methylated spirits and, if it is a fake, the beautiful blue tones will dissolve out almost immediately.

Another diamond trick is the fly-paper diamond, or stick-together diamond (called in the trade, a 'doublet'), a speciality confined mainly to Western Europe, where you find the greatest diamond-cutting craftsmen. It demands great technical skill, but this commodity may be had, like most things, for a high enough price.

At diamond-polishing workshops, when a diamond is ready for cutting, the top layer is cut off—about one-sixteenth of an inch of the original stone. This fragile slice may then be cut and polished into the semblance of a fine stone and, mounted on glass with a special glue, its depth and size can be made to appear truly fabulous. But it must be handled and sold in a setting, to ensure that inspection is possible only from the top, and the microscopic line of the craftsman's join to the glass base is invisible.

Seen from the top, the doublet diamond looks superb, and there are hundreds of them about the world to-day, still being sold and bought with exclamations of wonder and delight on both sides. A well-polished flypaper stone which costs the dealer about £80 can be sold for £500 with little trouble. Diamond buying, once the price is high, is a matter for experts only, and laymen should buy their stones from no one but the most reputable traders—any other deal must be suspect.

But even when the diamonds themselves are beyond question there enters the confidence man with his theatre of illusion and cunningly contrived situations. Perhaps the most subtle, and, indeed, the most successful plot, involves the outlay of thousands of pounds, and may be carried through only by the most presentable and astute of tricksters.

Only a few years ago a wealthy American entered a jeweller's shop in London's exclusive Bond Street and said he would like to buy a diamond. He viewed the dealer's stock and decided on a stone that was one of a pair.

The price for the two stones was £70,000, but the customer wanted only one of them. However, he understood the dealer's problem, and agreed to pay £40,000 for one of the diamonds. He wrote out a cheque immediately and asked the dealer to send him the diamond at his hotel—it happened to be the Dorchester, which is a fine address to have as a background for a deal like this, in the quiet, dignified calm of a really good jeweller's shop where even the doorman looks like an elder statesman and the salesmen themselves could be diplomats of the highest rank.

The diamond dealer was almost tempted to send the stone

without waiting to have the cheque cleared, but he did present it to the American's bank and was gratified to find it was not questioned in any way. He sent the stone to the Dorchester and, after a few weeks, the big sale had become nothing more than another satisfactory deal.

But there came a day, a few months later, when the £40,000 sale no longer seemed quite so satisfactory. Another customer, a Frenchman, appeared who wished to buy a pair of diamonds. It was, he explained a present for his wife, and from the way he said this it was quite obvious to the dealer that here was a problem which must be solved without delay. The customer in search of twin perfection for his wife, saw nothing that really excited him until his fine dark eyes lit upon the diamond so beautifully matched a few weeks ago but now, alas! a miserable solitaire.

"If you had a stone to match that, I should be satisfied," said the Frenchman. "But that, I suppose, is impossible?"

"I am afraid so, Sir," said the dealer in real anguish. "But we happen to know where the other stone is, and it is always possible that the gentleman may be prepared to let us have the stone back."

"Excellent," said the Frenchman. "Buy it from him. I will pay any price up to £80,000 if you can retrieve it. Please advise my secretary if you should have any success." He left a deposit of £10,000 on the other stone, for which he was prepared to pay £40,000 if the complete pair could be sold to him.

Hope dawned again in the dealer's beast. He contacted the first buyer and explained how desperately the new buyer wanted the two stones. The dealer said he would buy back the stone for £75,000. (If the proposition came off, the dealer would make an extra £5,000 for himself, on top of his legitimate profit.)

The dealer was delighted when the original buyer agreed to sell the stone back again, and sent him a certified cheque for £75,000. Next day the matching diamond was returned. The dealer telephoned the Frenchman's hotel. He had gone. He flew, only the day before, back to Paris, said the girl on the hotel switchboard. And the dealer never managed to contact the fond husband who wanted two diamonds for his wife.

Instead, the dealer had two matching diamonds, valued

fairly at £70,000 for which he had paid £75,000, plus their original purchase cost. True, he had £10,000 deposit on the second stone, which was never reclaimed, but the confidence men had £75,000 in return for the £40,000 they spent on the first stone, and the £10,000 deposit they left on the second. Thus they made a profit of £25,000. Not bad in the space of a few months. Good enough, in fact, to enable them to repeat their performance on some other diamond dealer who had priceless matched gems for sale and was not above being tempted into making a little more than his normal profit when the opportunity arose.

And what could the dealer have done? He took a perfectly normal business step in buying back a gem at an inflated price, knowing (or thinking he knew) that he had a buyer waiting who was prepared to pay an even higher sum. All the confidence men did was pay £40,000 for a diamond, place a £10,000 deposit on another, and sell the first one at a profit. Nothing dishonest there, was there? All they did was conjure up a highly inflated market for those two diamonds—and then let it collapse in the greedy dealer's lap.

Confidence men who deal in diamonds need a really smooth technique for they are operating in the most difficult branch of the confidence racket. A business man who succumbs to the tempation to increase his bank balance is relatively easy. But the man who deals in diamonds is supposed to know all the answers to the confidence man's approach.

And of all who deal in precious stones there is none shrewder than the pawnbroker. Yet even he can be tricked if the stage is carefully set and the swindle well performed.

Not long ago a well-dressed man of middle-age walked into a London pawnshop. It was in the early hours of trading and business was slack. He pulled from a black velvet purse two beautiful brooches with a large diamond set in the centre of each and two diamond bracelets and asked if a loan could be advanced on them. The assistant called his employer, an expert on fine stones, to examine them. The employer came from the rear of the shop, meticulously scrutinized the collection and valued them at £30,000. The loan the well-dressed man sought was a mere £12,000.

The pawnbroker explained to him that his credentials would

have to be checked as this was the usual procedure. The customer who gave his name as Colonel John Wykeham then gave the names of his bank, his club, and his stockbroker. He was asked to return next day with the jewels and if his credentials were satisfactory the deal would be concluded.

"I shall only want the money for twenty-four hours or so," he said as he left. "A small business transaction, you know. I'm sure you will find everything in order."

The bogus Colonel's credentials were, of course, perfectly sound. He and his accomplices had seen to that. When he returned to the shop next morning he handed over the jewels and departed with the £12,000 loan.

A month later he redeemed his property, saying blandly: "My transaction took a little longer than I expected." A few weeks later he was back again and asked if the loan could be repeated. The pawnbroker re-examined the jewels, declared he was satisfied and Colonel Wykeham left with the £12,000.

He repeated the process for three months and at the end of this time the pawnbroker, the assistant and the Colonel were on extremely friendly terms and jovially discussed the vicissitudes of big business which sometimes made such loans necessary. Throughout this period that he spent baiting the hook the Colonel always retained that reserve expected of a retired and respected Army officer. The assistant, especially, was suitably deferential to his well-mannered client.

There was nothing different on his last visit, except for one thing. He came in the lunch-hour and found that the pawnbroker, the expert on precious stones, was out at lunch.

"Oh, I am so sorry. What a pity!" he said to the assistant. Do you think I should wait . . .?"

"Not at all, Colonel, not at all. I'm sure it will be all right. How much, Sir . . . the same?"

"Yes, if you don't mind," said the Colonel and a few minutes later he walked into the crowded lunch-hour street leaving behind a collection of stones that were worth £1,000 at the most.

How had he done it? By simply replacing the large centre diamond in each brooch with beautiful but relatively inexpensive zircons. The settings were precisely the same and the bracelets he had left unchanged.

Only an expert could have told that the diamonds had gone and when, in fact, the pawnbroker did detect the switch a few hours later, it was too late.

The Colonel had vanished, counting a profit which, after deducting expenses, came to a cool £10,000.

At about the same time that Colonel Wykeham was dangling his bait in the London pawnshop a young, emaciated-looking man arrived at the Brussels Bourse to exploit the greed of blackmarket money dealers with a confidence trick that was both daringly simple and yet difficult to execute.

It called for only a short acting performance, lightning sleight of hand—and a fatalistic attitude to his future, for if he were caught he could expect little mercy from the ruthless money merchants who frequented the Bourse.

He told the tale that he was a Pole who had been interned in Russia and in his travels from Eastern Europe he had picked up a large quantity of American dollars. Most of them, he said, he "acquired" in Berlin. Were they worth much on the Belgian blackmarket?

The dealer whom he asked looked at the gaunt young man curiously, scarcely believing that he could possess a sum worth bothering about.

"I can offer you 50½ Belgian francs to the dollar," he said. "Take it or leave it."

The young man took from his pocket a bulging leather purse and peeled off 1,000 dollars in 100-dollar bills. The dealer looked closely at them expecting to toss them back as forgeries. But they were genuine enough and he gave the young man 50,000 Belgian francs in return, thereby gaining about 500 francs on the deal. The young man did not argue and the dealer congratulated himself on the small profit he had made from this unlikely source.

Ten days later the young Pole returned to the Bourse and hunted out his quarry. From his purse he drew another 1,000 dollars and the dealer examined them, happily repeated his profit-making transaction and muttered to himself that this was indeed a painless operation.

By now the young Pole had prepared his victim for the killing. The dealer took him for a "sucker", a raw recruit in a ruthless line of business. It was just the reaction the Pole had wanted.

His victim's business sense was dulled and if he had retained any emotional feeling in his emotionless profession it could only have been sympathy for the young Pole who was so easy to please.

The Pole struck late one afternoon when he met the dealer at the Bourse and said: "I have a much larger amount this time . . . 10,000 dollars. I want to open a business. This is too much money to handle on the streets. Could we go somewhere private?" His expression was that of a frightened animal, afraid that his booty might suddenly be seized from him by some mysterious adversary.

The dealer fell. He took the Pole to the apartment a few blocks away. The Pole produced his fat leather purse, his eyes darted apprehensively towards the door as though he expected an unwelcome intrusion. He counted out one hundred 100-dollar bills. Ten thousand dollars. The dealer checked it and returned the purse to the Pole while he began counting out the Belgian francs to give him in return.

It took only a second. While the dealer was occupied in counting out his part of the bargain the Pole slipped an identical purse onto the table and put the first one (still containing the dollars) back into his pocket. He did it with a swiftness and deftness of which any stage conjuror would have been proud.

He accepted the dealer's francs and hurried out . . . inside the purse he had left on the table were three 100-dollar bills wrapped around a wad of carefully-cut stationery.

You can buy the paper he used for his swindle at any Belgian stationer's for about five shillings a ream.

There is another rich vein of human frailty worked by confidence men. Snobbishness. Of all forms of snobbery, perhaps cultured snobbery is the most highly developed, and there is a mild old gentleman, living now in quiet and comfortable retirement in the south of France, who made this affectation among his fellows provide him with a livelihood and, eventually, security for his old age.

His name, of course, is not Ashlock, but that is the name he used the day he wandered in, a little vaguely, as befits the artistic temperament, to the picture dealer's in a street off

Piccadilly on a grey London afternoon. He unwrapped, with tender care, an old landscape in oils, a treasure he had picked up, he explained, during a recent holiday in Brussels. He had paid £500 for it.

The art dealer looked at the old man sharply. He did not look the sort of man who could pay a price like that for a painting, but one can never be sure about the English. The more money they have, some of them, the scruffier they look. Ashlock's rumpled tweeds and soft collar with its carelessly knotted tie, his slightly gnarled hands and his somewhat apologetic moustache indicated a man of only moderate means, and the picture was not one of the catalogued old masters. The dealer knew his paintings well enough to pick that.

"I wonder," the old man said timidly, "if you would be good enough to clean it for me. I have a feeling that it might well turn out to be a sixteenth century Italian masterpiece, although as far as I can see there is no sign of a signature. But the manner of the brushwork suggests the late seventeenth century."

The dealer looked at the picture doubtfully. "If you'd like it restored a little, Sir, I can have it done most expertly. But the fees for this sort of work these days are pretty stiff, you know."

"Oh, I don't mind paying a fair thing for professional work," Ashlock said mildly, "and in case you have any doubts about my integrity I can give you my references, my bank, my solicitor, and so on. I want to leave the picture here for some months as I am planning to settle abroad and, at the moment, I am existing in an hotel until I have my affairs more settled."

After a little further discussion about the picture, Ashlock left the gallery and the dealer watched him almost with pity. But he was not sure about the value of the painting. It looked old enough to be anything done by a competent craftsman, but it was not likely to be an old master, unless it was catalogued, and this, the dealer was quite certain, was not the case.

When the picture was restored, it had a certain charm that had not been apparent before, and the dealer kept it on his wall in his main showroom, where he passed it off on many of his customers as a genuine masterpiece. He derived much innocent amusement from the ready acceptance of the old man's picture as a valuable work of art by people who pretended to know the period thoroughly. By the time the American widow came in and 'fell in love' with the picture, the dealer was quite used to pretending it was one of Europe's hitherto undisclosed treasures, with a market value of perhaps £25,000.

Other customers had inquired its price, but in a casual manner. They had merely been interested as connoisseurs, not as buyers. The American woman was a buyer, and she was in search of something remarkable to bear back to her home-town in triumph, a cultural conquest that would be the envy of her friends, and a permanent memorial to her own taste and knowledge of the arts.

"How much for that picture I hear you've discovered? That masterpiece that's never been catalogued? A little man at my hotel says it's an incredible find." She was a commanding woman and she moved in an aura of wealth that brought every businesslike instinct in the picture dealer's body to the alert.

"Unfortunately, Madam, it is not for sale. I am merely custodian of the picture and, you realize, its authenticity has not yet received official recognition."

"Look, that's the picture I want," the American said. Difficulties merely roused her determination. "You think £30,000 would buy it? Well, anyway, here's £5,000 as deposit just to show you I'm serious about this."

The dealer suppressed a delighted smile and said he would get in touch with the owner and see what he could do. When he did manage to speak to Ashlock a day or so later the old man was not at all interested in selling his picture at first. But the dealer finally persuaded him on the ground that a gallery in the United States were anxious to have it and that, apart from the £25,000 they were prepared to pay (again the trader had stepped in to gain a little extra reward), it would be a generous action to allow the picture to be shared by thousands instead of locking it up in a private home.

Reluctantly, the old man agreed. He was not particularly interested when the dealer explained that ten per cent of the price would be deducted as agent's commission, and he tucked the dealer's cheque for £22,500 into his worn leather wallet with no show of pleasure at all.

Too simple a device to hoodwink an experienced dealer? It seems so, when one reads it in the knowledge that we are presenting examples of the confidence racket, but it happened.

It was worked successfully by the so-called Ashlock on many occasions, because he knew about pictures. His fakes were never presented as anything but "bargains" he had dredged up himself in remote European art shops, and he did not even have to exploit the snobbery of art collectors with more money than taste—he left that to his good friends, the dealers.

His own appearance was a consummate imitation of the serious connoisseur, slightly careless in his dress, mild and absorbed in his particular and scholarly enthusiasm for sixteenth century paintings. But it was only after he had passed their way that the dealers in half a dozen capital cities in Europe realized that Ashlock was not only a connoisseur of painting, he was a connoisseur of human nature as well. His "interesting old paintings" seldom cost him more than a couple of hundred pounds, his living expenses were necessarily modest to remain in keeping with his role as a devoted student of the arts, and through the years his bank balance grew steadily to provide him with all the comfort he required for his declining years.

On a less delicately subtle level is the story of the Persian carpet sellers—the widespread tribe of confidence men who operate on the humble ground of door-to-door salesmanship in some countries, and as smart traders in a luxury business in others.

The remarkable thing about the carpet crooks is that so many of them are Dutchmen. A lot, however, are (or claim to be) Viennese or Hungarian. It was one of the latter nationality, *The Hungarian Baron*, who gave the best illustration yet of what a confidence man could do with a carpet.

The Baron's story, with subtle variations according to mood and circumstances, of course, was that he was a displaced Hungarian Baron who escaped from his country with nothing from his family estates near Debreczyn but a few crates of priceless Persian carpets. These glowing tapestries of colour and skill, the Baron explained had originally belonged to the Polish Monarch Jan Sobieski, a seventeenth century hero who defeated the Turks at the siege of Vienna, and had returned heavily laden with looted carpets from his victorious expedition.

The Baron sold his so-called Persian carpets to expert traders in England, convincing them partly by his own air of integrity and enlisting a certain amount of sympathy for his plight in the years immediately after World War I. But he also had the sagacity to produce a most impressive file of papers—letters of valuation from Continental experts, customs' invoices, transit dockets, fake histories of the carpets on suitably crested writing paper, and references to them in other letters, which mentioned details about the carpets only as incidental information among other reports of thousands of acres of spruce and fir, or farming lands, and the fate of costly plate and family jewels. Everything about the Baron had an air of exotic wealth, of lost fortunes and noble birth tragically reduced to little importance in a changing world.

The Baron's insurance against retribution was based, as the con. man's security is so often based, on the knowledge that his victims—experts in their own right—would never be likely to admit that they had been tricked, but would pass the spurious goods on as rapidly as possible to their more gullible customers. The world's "Persian" carpets would cover all of Persia's barren acres—if only they were genuine!

There is a regular international trade in Persian carpets, but not all are supplied with the pedigree the Baron gave his choice selection. Most are bought by a central distributor in each country and supplied by shrewd buyers of Italian and Belgian carpeting who know just how Persian a carpet needs to look to be sold under false colours.

The main dealers parcel their wares out to travelling salesmen who exploit the country towns, the lonely farmsteads (outside of which their cars so often and so conveniently break down), and the prosperous small town merchants who feel that a priceless Persian floor-covering will give them the social standing they so anxiously desire to impress their friends and neighbours.

The Baron, a large, portly European aristocrat, with a monocle and an air of indefinable sadness, occasioned, no doubt, by the cruel necessity of having to sell his large stock of £70 carpets for £1,200 apiece, finally ran out of his stock. He is now employed by a reputable carpet firm as a buyer and, although his life is now untroubled by fear of exposure as a charlatan, it is safe and prosperous—and he never buys a Persian carpet.

Some of the tricks confidence men play are unbelievably crude when put down in black and white, but these men are not working with logical, law-abiding citizens when they pull their cruder stunts. Hoodwinking an honest man calls for a vastly different technique from fleecing a crook. If a man's money has been gained dishonestly he is far more likely to stake it in a gamble that is a little shady, and far less likely to complain effectively if he has been robbed.

Confidence men throughout the world come to know each other by repute, and there exists among those of them who travel widely, a kind of loose liaison, a bond of mutual interest, which results in their lending each other funds to tide over tough spots, and the sharing of tips and advice for fellow tradesmen operating in different sections of the market. The man who can convince businessmen that he can put them in the way of a quick market profit would no more try to sell old paintings to art dealers than fly—or do an honest day's work. And the remarkable little group who work the "magic box" trick would never dream of trying it on anyone but a crook with a wallet full of black money.

It is so crudely a bait for greedy, stupid men, this magic box trick, that it is almost unbelievable. But it works over and over again. Even now, at this minute, some simple criminal is probably being approached by a man he knows is a forger. The forger is not suggesting a deal in the usual way, but says he has come across a "nut", an inventor, who has perfected a photo-electric reproduction machine which can produce perfect paper money.

The forger takes his victim in tow after a few drinks and invites him to come and see the money machine for himself. It is always a few blocks away, in a furtive, shabby part of town—the sort of area where a poor man is likely to live, unwanted and rejected by the world.

When the forger and his friend arrived at the "inventor's" room they find a large box-shaped assortment of containers, cameras, lights and spools of film and paper, all arranged on a rickety wooden table. The "inventor", pale and thin and talking excitedly about his technical triumphs, hardly bothers to acknowledge the presence of his visitors. But the forger explains the set-up. The victim produces a crisp, clean 100 dollar bill from his wallet and feeds it into the machine. The "inventor" presses a few levers, throws a switch and the whole contraption begins to whirr and vibrate. The forger opens a hatch at the bottom of the machine and brings out not one, but *five* 100-dollar bills. It is as easy as that!

It is further explained to the victim that the machine, because of some intricate limitation in its workings, can reproduce only four fake notes for each original fed into it.

"It's put me out of work, that damn machine," the forger says ruefully. "And until we can find a guy with a new supply of clean 100-dollar bills we can't clean up on the thing."

It is suggested to the victim that he might like to take the machine's notes to a bank to have them checked. This he does, and comes hastening back to say that the notes were accepted without hesitation as true currency. Would he like to be in a major coup with the machine then? The poor chap can hardly contain his excitement and delight.

When the new boy has managed to assemble 5,000 dollars in 100-dollar notes, clean and crisp, he is allowed to feed them into the magic machine himself. The "inventor" presses his levers and starts his machine.

Suddenly, amid the whirring, there is a grating noise, and before anyone can move, the whole machine erupts in a sheet of searing flame and smoke. The room is about to become an inferno of crackling heat when the forger, with great presence of mind, flings the "inventor's" bedclothes over the blaze and the men retreat, coughing and weeping, to the landing, their lungs bursting with smoke.

They fight their way back inside, desperate to retrieve something from the wreck, but the machine is a shapeless mass of twisted, heated metal. The money has obviously been destroyed, and the victim gets nothing but sympathy from his forger friend.

The "inventor" is distraught. When the victim has left, the "inventor" gropes beneath the table and unclasps the fireproof asbestos box in which the good money is safely resting—and the magic printing machine trick has worked again.

There are risks in the magic box routine which few confidence men will accept. Magic box operators are regarded about as respectfully, compared to financial crooks, in the Underworld, as plumbers are compared to surgeons in the normal world.

The better class of con. men create their situations from the weaknesses of people, invent their backgrounds and carry out their business without being encumbered by a shred of material evidence.

Should anything go wrong, they deny everything, disappear without leaving a trace, or, in some cases, blandly advise the injured parties to go ahead and call in the machinery of the law. Their elaborate schemes can be abandoned with no loss but the loss of their time spent in creating a false sense of security in the victim, and the slight inconvenience of being known unfavourably to yet another of the world's honest citizens.

In the Underworld, the confidence men are the aristocrats. But the Underworld has big business executives, too, and it is among these criminal types that we find the men who direct the drug traffic, the prostitution rackets, the gambling networks, and the powerful protection groups who extort vast tribute from unions. They prey on the weak and the frightened, and the foolish who try to escape from reality by courting luck or by forgetting their problems in lust.

Confidence men operate alone or, occasionally, in pairs. The other denizens of the Underworld tend to work in groups, restless, ruthless packs, owing temporary allegiance to leaders as brutalized and depraved as any humans can be. It is to some of these types that we now turn in our attempt to understand the constant menace of crime.

We are not attempting to do anything more in this survey of confidence tricks than mention a few of the thousands of ruses that have been, and are employed to fool the public; some are elaborate and demand great patience and big resources, some are simple and quick—so simple that no man in his right mind would take them seriously. Perhaps that is why they work so well.

3

pickpockets

SAY the word "pickpocket" to an Englishman and he knows exactly what you mean. He imagines a shabby, furtive fellow lurking in a football or race-track crowd, loitering about a busy market-place on the lookout for a slightly tipsy man with an unbuttoned coat, or a wallet sticking out from a hip-pocket. Pickpockets, to the Englishman, are little more than nimble sneak-thieves, whose rewards are small and whose risk is great. Pickpockets are not taken very seriously in Britain.

This picture of the pickpocket could hardly be further from the truth. The true pickpocket is well-dressed and presentable, the sort of man who would be above suspicion should anyone raise the ugly cry of "Stop thief!" Pickpockets are highly organized, have special rules of behaviour and ethics and an international understanding greater than any other criminal community.

It is a "profession" that is acquired only after years of arduous practice, experience and faithful adherence to the pickpocket's rigid code. Their co-operation, their discipline and their loyalty to each other have developed from the peculiar needs of the trade and, apart from these practical considerations, is entirely voluntary.

Pickpockets are individualists. Their profession calls for constant imagination and improvization, close observation of their fellow humans and, in the case of the well-established operators, assets like faked travel documents and reliable contacts with the police. The trade is highly skilled. It calls for courage, an ability to make quick, bold decisions and a cool nerve to carry them out without loss of poise.

The successful pickpockets of Europe and South American countries (the profession thrives best in these areas, for reasons shortly to be explained) are often men of substance and property, well-to-do citizens with a family background of comfort and responsibility and every reason in the world to avoid trouble at all costs. Their stake in a career of successful crime is far too valuable to risk by careless or crude behaviour. If they come under suspicion, they are by no means at the end of their resources—they hire the best lawyers and make any "arrangements" that may be possible with the local police and legal authorities.

A master pickpocket from Brussels visited Britain last year. He travelled, as usual, first class. His papers were beyond suspicion and, well-groomed and graciously mannered, he had no difficulty in being accepted as a respectable guest at a good hotel in the Strand. He had come to do a little business in London, partly because he liked a change of scene and partly because he knew it would be unwise to be seen for a while in Paris, Berlin, Rome and other European cities, normally his regular haunts.

But his English venture was not a success. After ten "fixes" (the pickpocket's professional term for each job undertaken) he confessed that he was bitterly disappointed. His total takings were £8 3s. 6d. in cash and three books of stamps! The unspeakable English, he said, carried no money. They were so dismally orderly in their public behaviour that they seldom gave a man a chance to bump up against them (or if one *did* collide with another man in the street, the incident was regarded as almost amounting to an assault!) and they wore their clothes so tightly buttoned that it almost needed a crowbar to get at their pockets. The Brussels expert was disheartened and angry. He had risked ruining his whole unblemished career for the sake of a few miserable pounds and his professional pride was sorely wounded. There was only one thing to do and he did it—he left by the next plane for Paris, to a country where a man of enterprise and special skill could make a decent living.

On the Continent, he explained, people are human. They get excited in crowds, they push and struggle to clamber on buses and trains. London's maddeningly patient queues (in which the slightest departure from meek and patient behaviour earned him the coldest of stares) really shattered his hopes. On the Continent people carry money in their wallets, not just a pound or so. Cheques, the man from Brussels added, are not used nearly as much in Europe as they are in Britain.

Business people in France and Germany, Italy and Belgium, do not want to be journeying to and from banks all the time. The more transactions carried out in cash, the less chance is there of their finances becoming known to the income tax authorities. And, after all, a man's financial affairs are strictly his own business and not to be shared with a lot of prying officials.

There is another great virtue (for the pickpocket) in Continental ways. It is possible to create a disturbance, to pick a quarrel or to start a jostling, noisy argument on the slightest pretext. A pickpocket has a chance to set the scene for his *fixes*. And when he does decide to go to work he has a reasonable chance of reaping a decent reward for the risk he takes and the skill he possesses.

Although the penalties for picking pockets in England are not as severe as they are on the Continent, the take is so small that the risks are not worth while. No, he had learned one lesson in England—it is no place for any pickpocket of any professional standing. Why, a lifetime of expert operation might be destroyed for the sake of wallet containing a season ticket on a train and a couple of football pool coupons. He would not feel easy, he said, until he was back in the crowded Metro in Paris.

Pickpockets have two main divisions in their labour, the actual thieving and the decoy work. Some really specialized pickpocketing groups consist of as many as five operators, each with an allotted and carefully defined task. Seldom does a Continental or South American pickpocket work alone.

The European trade name for pickpockets is *urkers*, the Russian term for these light-fingered adventurers. They are also known as *pukiels*, a term which covers the helpers. The *urker* (or *dip*, or *hooker*) is regarded as by no means the most important member of the pilfering syndicate. The valuable work is done by the decoys whose task it is to "easy up" the victim, to create a situation and distract his attention. These performers, on whose ability the success of the operation mainly depends, are sometimes called the *Titzer*, or "bunch". Really efficient and enterprising Titzers do three-quarters of the work. By the time they have "eased up" the victim they should have the loot pretty well presented on a platter.

Shortly before the second World War when professionals made all Europe their hunting ground, one of the most efficient gangs was composed of a "hooker" and three *Titzers*. On arrival in a big town this particular gang would first go to a bank and, splitting up as they entered, would study the layout, note the number of people and select a likely victim.

When one of the team saw a man who had drawn a large amount from the bank he would signal the others and follow him outside. If the man entered a bus or a tram the Titzers would close in and provide a "Squeeze"—a sudden jostling of the victim and the hooker. (A similar distraction could be engineered if the man walked.)

In a moment the hooker would do his work, using a razor blade to cut away the side of the man's attaché case (or, if he happened to have tucked it firmly under one arm, the end would be slit.). The moment the money was extracted, the gang would vanish in the crowd before the theft was noticed. The next day they would be at work in another town.

On one occasion they picked a likely victim, but found that he stepped into a waiting car as soon as he left the bank. The gang considered the situation. They decided the man had been drawing out wages for his staff; it was the right day of the week and the combination of notes and silver the man had demanded from the teller indicated this was the purpose of his withdrawal. They bought a bag exactly like the one their prospective victim carried and, when the next pay-day came around they were in the bank, ready to strike. Their bag was filled with paper and stones to match the weight of the bag they planned to switch.

They had worked out their getaway with great care, for this is the most important part of almost every pickpocketing operation. One of the *Titzers* was detailed to stand by and take the man's bag when it was switched. Another member of the gang, who was standing immediately behind him as he collected the money, waited until the victim placed the bag between his feet and began buttoning up his coat and putting on his gloves. The *Titzer* tapped the man on the shoulder and asked him a question.

The victim turned to answer, the hooker switched the bags, scooped up the man's bag and moved a few feet away to pass it to his waiting colleague. In a matter of seconds the stolen bag was outside and the four pickpockets followed. There had been nothing hurried in their movements, everything was done casually to match the somewhat dignified tempo normal to banking business.

The plan worked perfectly and the robbed man did not even suspect his loss until he reached his own office. By then it was too late for him to hope to do anything about the gang who would be on their way to another town by car or train within minutes of leaving the bank.

If anything went wrong with the operation, a gang like this would throw the stolen goods away before the police caught up with them. Even if caught without the loot, the police might make trouble and they would take any risks to avoid arrest. Once apprehended and questioned, the gang's identity would be recorded carefully and circulated widely by the police who kept extensive dossiers on the known pickpockets in most Continental towns and cities. Once this happened, a gang's field of operations would be seriously limited.

Somewhere in South America to-day there lives a man who, for daring and icy nerve, was rarely equalled even in the early thirties, that heyday for the modern pickpocket. The Great Lekovici, as this Rumanian gentleman styled himself in the days of his bigger triumphs, started off humbly enough. He was bred in the pickpocket trade and, with the lessons he learned in it, graduated to a robbery that remains a *cause célèbre* in the annals of the underworld.

He lives now in a sumptuous villa in an exclusive hillside suburb overlooking a busy city. He does not work for a living in the sense that you and I do. His "working day" consists largely of tedious rounds of golf followed by a martini or two, a swim in his private swimming pool and a respectable (and honest) evening at cards.

For the means that provided most of this flashy luxury the Great Lekovici can look back to one grey, cloudy morning in Berlin. It was 1921. Berlin was a Hell's Kitchen of criminals ranging from the minor street bullies to the mean play-for-keeps razor slashers and gunslingers.

Lekovici's big moment that day in 1921 was, like all coups of its kind, alarmingly simple.

For weeks, Lekovici and two *Titzers* had watched the

movements of a small band of soldiers of the Reichswehr who, once a week, at precisely the same time drove up to the central office of the Reichsbank and collected army pay for the Berlin garrison.

The robbery had to be perfectly timed. They had to be certain of when the truck arrived at the bank; the number of soldiers who emerged; who carried the sacks into which the money would be stowed; how long it took for the teller to hand over the cash; the number of staff in the bank; an approximate number of the customers at that time.

On the chosen day the Army truck pulled up as usual but exactly ten seconds after the soldiers had entered the bank a small car nosed into an adjacent parking spot. Out of it came three men in the uniforms of non-commissioned officers of the Reichswehr. They boldly strode into the bank, nodded curtly to the private who stood near the door and headed for the little knot of men at the Receiving counter.

There, Reichsmarks were being stuffed into a large canvas bag, about the size of a sugar bag. The Great Lekovici approached the solder who was superintending this operation and uttered a few non-committal remarks. The soldier listened politely and then conscientiously returned to the task of seeing that the money was stowed into the bags. But Lekovici was persistent. "This damn garrison life gets you down after a while doesn't it?" he said. "I wish to God something would happen." He then railed on about the monotony of such an existence with such enthusiasm that the soldier simply had to take notice.

While they talked the stowing of the money was completed. Lekovici's uniformed accomplices calmly picked up the bag and lugged it outside. They stowed it into the car, waited until the Great Lekovici appeared, followed by the soldiers from the truck. Lekovici stepped into the car, the soldiers into the truck and everyone drove off happily. Happily, that is, until when the truck arrived at the garrison camp and its passengers found they had been robbed of a fortune.

Astounding as this episode appears it really did happen. It called for nerves of steel and a staggering amount of cheek by Lekovici and his two accomplices in thinking they could get away with it. And that is just what they did.

One of the most experienced pickpockets in recent times was

a Polish woman who went to Australia after the war with her husband, who always helped her in her work. A middle-aged matron with two grown sons, she was regarded as one of the best razor-operators in the business. She specialized in robbing people at the races and could slice a man's hip pocket or vest pocket open with the delicate touch of a surgeon. To cut just the right thickness of cloth in such cases demands a polished skill.

Her method was so outstandingly brilliant that police in Sydney soon realized a visiting professional was at work. They kept a careful watch for several months. Finally they caught her, but she skipped bail and left the country on a forged passport to return to Europe. She was caught, a few months later, while working with her husband and two other men in Brussels and sentenced to five years' gaol.

Pickpockets who survive long enough in their trade to become experts are professionals to whom no detail is too slight to consider and no amount of trouble too great in the pursuit of a perfect performance. Not only honest geniuses know that an infinite capacity for taking pains is the secret of success! But even the most experienced *hookers* can make mistakes. Two lone-operators robbed each other on one occasion in a crowded underground station and as it happened, came off almost even. It took them a long time to live this blunder down when their friends came to discover the incident in the course of the ceaseless gossip that circulates in criminal circles.

First-class pickpockets are master craftsmen who plan each *fix* in minute detail. They operate as the leaders of well-disciplined teams and make a handsome living as a result. They work in different fields, have dozens of different approaches and perfect various specialities. In the trade, however, there are three recognized territories of operation, each with its own experts. There are market-place operators and about-town operators (trams, buses, trains, theatres, lifts, railway stations and ships); razor-blade operators (a very highly-skilled branch of the profession); and bank operators (who must have an impeccable front and nerves of steel).

The bank operators include the most intelligent and highly skilled experts who are by far the most prosperous members of the profession. It takes a good actor to present himself as a bank pickpocket and one of these, who always worked alone, was a man of most distinguished appearance. He led a blameless life as a family man in Budapest, raised two sons to be doctors and married his daughter well, without ever being apprehended. The risks he took would make any ordinary man grow cold with fear.

Perhaps the greatest artists in the pickpocket business in Europe were the refugee Russians who became famous between the two World Wars. But they were closely rivalled by Rumanian and Hungarian *urkers* and, some people maintain, even bettered by the best of the Chilean experts.

The pickpockets in Chile have a world (or perhaps we should say "underworld"?) reputation for skill, organizing ability, almost incredible dexterity and a boundless courage. Their slim fingers develop a lightness of touch the victim never feels or sees and it is sometimes difficult to make them believe they have been robbed. They are sure they must have lost their wallets or cash only by their own carelessness.

Some sections of the underworld consider that Polish pickpockets have a greater intelligence, a deeper brilliance in selecting and planning their *fixes*, than any other nationality. Polish operators travel more widely and more freely than any of their colleagues. They have a facility for procuring false papers that no one can better and their capacity for work is phenomenal. Perhaps it is because conditions in Poland have always been so severe. The Polish pickpockets, who sometimes, in their early years as *urkers*, have to pick twenty pockets to acquire a decent haul, are always on the go and move about very successfully without becoming known in any one place.

One of the most successful pickpockets was a lone wolf, a single-handed dip who went by the underworld name of Bobbinek and never worked anywhere but at railway stations. To his fellows he was known by his habit of standing at a station, an overcoat over his cunning right arm, while he sized up likely victims in the passing crowds. But even Bobbinek, for all his experience and shrewd observation, once had an unlucky streak in which he acquired little more than loose change in twenty-five jobs.

The normal person finds it hard to understand how a man like Bobbinek could exist for long as a railway station pickpocket without being caught and punished. Surely, these law-abiding people argue, such a man would spend more time in prison than out of it and he would become so well-known to the police that he could never hope to be left alone long enough to carry out his plans. Pickpockets, it should be remembered, make their dishonest living from just such people as these—people who cannot imagine how a pickpocket gets way with his thieving.

There are two things which make the Bobbineks of the underworld possible. One, and by far the most important of the two reasons for prosperous pickpocketing, is the general behaviour of the public, especially the travelling public. The other is the strange (?) reluctance of the police in some countries to arrest pickpockets on sight.

Experienced pickpockets, like Bobbinek, owe a great deal of their success to their commonplace appearance. They are "average" men, moderately tall, reasonably dressed, quiet of manner and they acquire an ability to be in a crowded place for hours on end without attracting the slightest attention.

A properly trained pickpocket will not dream of trying to steal from an obviously alert citizen carrying only one case with the air of a man who knows just where he is going. But railway station crowds always provide a fair sprinkling of worried travellers—elderly people who are hastening to catch a train with only seconds to spare, harrassed people with a lot of luggage and, maybe, one or two children to manage as well.

A great deal of the art of successful pickpocketing lies in judging just how soon it will be before the victim checks his purse or his wallet or his packages and thus discovers he has been robbed. Think for a moment, how often the average man or woman feels to make sure his wallet is intact, or looks in her purse to count its contents.

Only the most nervous and timid of travellers are forever putting their hands in their pockets to make sure they have not lost their money. Only the most suspicious of travellers keep counting their luggage as they make their way to their trains. No sensible pickpocket is going to take an unnecessary risk by trying to steal from these people.

The bustling, crowded scene at a railway station provides dozens of opportunities for a skilful *urker* to move in on his victim without appearing to behave oddly. There is, also, another protective device the pickpocket uses—if he is skilled, he will not take all a man's money, he will not remove all his jewellery or take all his packages. If a man has a roll of notes in his pocket, the expert thief will extract it, peel off a few notes, and return the only slightly thinner roll to the victim's pocket. And when the poor fellow feels to see if his roll is still there he is quite reassured to discover that it is. It is not until much later that he finds not all of his money is there.

By stealing with restraint the professional *dip* allows a further doubt to creep into the victim's mind—perhaps the missing article was left at home. This doubt is a further valuable protection for the thief.

This sort of limited stealing takes a great deal of self-control, but it pays big dividends over a long period and pickpockets of this type have not spent years acquiring their special skills just for the sake of a few quick robberies. They are in the business for life, and even one arrest will undo years of careful work.

The practice of peeling off a few notes and leaving the rest is a rule that is often closely followed by bank operators who will watch a man withdraw, say, £100 and then take only £30 or £40 of it, leaving the victim quite sure that his money has not been touched. And if a pickpocket can disappear from the scene immediately after he has struck, the bewildered victim may forever believe that his loss was due to his own carelessness or forgetfulness.

The fewer people who realize they have been robbed, the better it is in the long run for the pickpocketing brotherhood. It would be interesting to know just how many people who have lost money or possessions while they have been travelling put their loss down to the correct cause.

Every country, of course, has its own "native breed" of pickpocket for only local types can hope to appear inconspicuous in market-places, banks and in public vehicles. Strangers, however, can operate with almost as much freedom at race-tracks, in hotels and on railway stations because in these places one takes no particular notice of strangers.

The best known and the most dangerous of all pickpockets, however, are those who travel about as men of the world, smart, urbane and charming in any company at any time. For them the field is always fresh, the supply of new victims endless as they roam from city to city. In many cases these roving professionals have forged documents and thus develop a close liaison with another branch of the underworld, the forgers. International pickpockets exchange information on where to find the best document fakers, advise each other on prices for these valuable wares and do a great deal of exchanging of papers among themselves. There is no formal relationship between the forgers of documents and the pickpockets, but both groups are indispensable to each other.

Most pickpockets stay in *Melinas* (see Chapter 4), the part-brothel, part-rooming house establishments run by retired prostitutes or procurers, when they come to a new city. Their knowledge of each other grows as the years go by and the constant stream of information that flows among them enriches their experience and increases their cunning enormously.

Which police are "approachable", which beats are done to death, what big public occasions are coming, where stolen property may be sold safely, who has been caught and how—all these snippets of gossip add up to a formidable intelligence service.

The unsuspecting public goes blithely about its business on the look-out for entirely the wrong type of suspicious character. It is the down-at-heel, obviously criminal type for whom the average man keeps a watch and not the well-groomed and even considerate fellow whose appearance is beyond reproach. It is, of course, the obviously dishonest types who appear so often in court and this fact serves to confirm the honest citizen in his erroneous belief that he "can always pick a crook". These much-arrested ne'er-do-wells are punished over and over again for their clumsy and minor thefts, while the skilled operators go free.

The pickpocketing community know hundreds of their fellows by nick-names, but seldom by their true names. Although there are, naturally, no written lists of membership of the profession, prominent members are known and recognized by other pickpockets all over the world. They have, also, a strict code of behaviour and a strong sense of what is the "done-thing" and what is considered outrageous behaviour.

It is never done, for instance, to inform the police about other members of the group; it is not done to prey on another man's territory or in any way hamper a colleague's "fix". There are even international "Honour Courts" in which men who break the rules are punished and quarrels are settled among gang members.

Most complaints that come before the so-called Honour Courts concern charges that a gang member has not turned over the full loot. This temptation is a constant one when one member lifts the loot after others have organized the fix and then scattered in different directions without waiting to see just what the result of the job has been.

One classic case of this type of suspicion arose when a man called Krovak the Claw (he had unsightly curved fingernails) and his team had worked for weeks to arrange the robbery of a bank messenger in Prague. The messenger had been relieved of a fat envelope of high denomination currency (and a worthless packet placed in his coat pocket) after a squabble in the street. All had appeared to go well. But, after the accomplices had disappeared, police chased the *urker* and he was forced to dart into a hotel lavatory and flush the money down a lavatory to escape being caught with the evidence of the crime.

The rest of the gang waited patiently for The Claw to meet them and share out the proceeds of the job, but he did not turn up. The next day there was a paragraph in the papers reporting the theft and it was said the messenger had lost *two* packages of the bank's money, totalling the equivalent of £3,000. Only The Claw knew that the messenger was taking the opportunity to make a little haul for himself, because only one envelope had been lifted, although The Claw's sensitive fingers had touched both packets in the man's pocket.

When The Claw told his story to the gang, they refused to believe him. They might have stomached the loss of one packet of money, or chosen to have believed it was jettisoned during a chase by the police, but the thought of losing two packets of cash just on the word of The Claw was too much for them. The Claw was severely beaten and, to make his plight worse, re-arrested by the police who reasoned that he would never have been molested unless he had had something to hide from the gang. Thieves are the last people to believe that there is honour among thieves.

Honour Courts, however, do not normally hand out beatings for defaulters. All they want is a fair share of the money and the usual penalties are large fines. The courts also arrange for the payment of grants to families of pickpockets who are imprisoned so that they will suffer no extreme hardship; they also have funds to pay legal fees when a gang member pleads not guilty, or appeals against a conviction.

One of the most brilliant pickpockets in Eastern Europe between the wars was a dark, motherly woman known in the trade as The Golden Hand. She was a razor-blade technician who specialized in meeting migrants returning from America.

Rushing through the dockside crowds, or shoving her way to the front of railway station groups, the Golden Hand would embrace one of the homecoming Poles, Lithuanians or Rumanians with a great show of tearful joy. She would hug him close, then hold him away from her at arm's length to inspect him more carefully just like any distraught mother re-united after many years with her loved ones. Before the surprised migrant could be quite sure that this was a case of mistaken identity and start to explain (as gently as possible, for the Golden Hand's emotion was most sincere and touching) that she was clasping the wrong son to her bosom, the lining of his coat would have been skilfully gutted of all the hard-won dollars he was smuggling home.

When she was not meeting long-lost relatives, the Golden Hand operated on women victims in trains, boats and hotels with incredible daring and cunning. She was a mistress of her trade and had the peeling-off technique down to a fine art. Her ability to pick and choose her victims earned her an almost legendary fame among other professionals. She was an "all-rounder"—an *urker* who could operate from any angle to gain access to any pocket from inner-vest to hip and explore the possibilities of linings and hems and belts as well. The Golden Hand is still operating, but not in Europe. She now lives in Buenos Aires and teams with her lover.

The worst thing that can happen to a European pickpocket is to become known to Interpol, the international police system. Interpol has lists of all types of criminals who have been convicted three times, and, once a man is listed, he must keep moving and always be on the alert.

Britain and America are not popular hunting grounds for pickpockets—Britain is too orderly and America imposes extremely heavy penalties—but there are parts of Canada where pickpockets seem to have come to terms with the police and the pickings are good. The old days of gang supremacy in the United States, when almost every town had a *fix* organized with the police, are over since the Federal sleuths took over from State police. But South American countries are a gold mine for skilled operators.

The outstanding advantage about being a pickpocket is that work is always at hand and there are no tools of trade apart from nimble fingers and shrewd judgment. It is a profession in which one may start young, the younger the better, and one is too old only when one is bedridden. Indeed, advancing years add to a pickpocket's chances of success. People are much more tolerant of the stumblings and blunderings of old people in a crowd than they are of the same antics by younger people, and many a veteran *dip* has exacted his tribute from well-meaning men and women who have been kind enough to aid him across a busy street.

Every occasion which brings people together in crowds gives the pickpocket an opportunity to go to work, and whether it is a wedding or a funeral, it makes no difference to a skilled man. Public grief and public joy are regarded as bonuses by the expert. He can operate so much more easily when his victims are already distracted.

The most valuable of all distractions, of course, is a pretty woman. Women with charm, and cool enough nerve to become skilled professionals, can remove a wallet as they yield to a kiss, or gently peel a few notes off a man's roll as they snuggle a little closer in his arms on a park bench. Women pickpockets have an infallible asset in their attractiveness. It breaks down all caution in their male victim. In lifts, crowded buses and trains and in dance-halls, the women *dips* operate with lightning skill. The lady-killer who fancies he is making yet another romantic conquest presents his money and valuables to the women pickpocket as though he were handing them to her on a platter. And if she is not helping herself to this easy harvest, you may be sure her accomplice is doing so under the cover of her fluttering eyelashes and coy advances.

To the normal person, crowds are just masses of people. But to the artists of the pickpocketing business they are an array of prospects as easy to rifle as an unguarded Christmas tree. Whether they are working, or merely resting between jobs, the pickpocket's eyes are summing up every stranger he meets, observing his movements, noting his dress and mentally assessing the contents of his wallet. A good operator can value a watch at ten paces to within a few shillings of its actual price, he can pick just where a man carries his paper money and he knows enough about clasps, pins and fastening of jewellery to write a book on the subject.

At any given moment, the expert could tell you how that man in the brown suit would react to having his toe trodden on, how that woman in the furs and blue hat would behave if she were accosted as a long lost friend, how hard that trim matron would let you lean on her in a crowded lift and how easy it would be to explore that young man's hip pocket if you stood beside him for a moment to share his scrutiny of a shop window. The sizing up of prospects goes on in a pickpocket's mind as steadily and automatically as you and I breathe and walk. For these professional criminals their life is their art and all the world is ripe for picking. They select only the easy victims, choose only the most convenient moments and they seldom make mistakes.

Closely allied to the pickpocket, both in mentality and skill, is the shoplifter. There is, these days, a popular conception of shoplifters. They are generally, so the story goes, amateurs who have a strange compulsion to steal from stores. In most cases, one reads, these people have no need to steal. They do it merely for excitement or to make up for a feeling of not being loved, or because they derive a sense of power and cunning from their petty thefts. All this may be true of the petty shoplifter, but with the professionals it is a different story.

Shoplifters have a definite place in the underworld. They have not the exalted standing of the confidence man or the same skilful status as the pickpocket, but they are still high in the scale of underworld class-distinction. They never operate in crowded department stores. They leave this highly dangerous field to the amateurs and the genuine, as well as the pretended, kleptomaniacs. Big stores are well guarded and customers are too closely watched by staff detectives to make their counters attractive to the professional shoplifter. They seldom have anything worth stealing anyway, at least that is what the professionals think.

The only shoplifter the underworld recognizes is the diamond and jewel thief who makes his light-fingered living by taking enormous risks. The risks of detection are enormous because the diamond shoplifter does not steal from the gullible public, but from men and women who are supposed to be experts in guarding their valuable stock.

One of the essential resources a shoplifter must have is a wide and reliable contact with his fellow criminals in several countries. Mobility, rapid travel from city to city, is another basic condition of success among the high-level shoplifting group and they often use forged papers to maintain their security. They must also have all the other facilities the underworld provides for its members—safe bases from which to size up a prospective job, accommodation protected from the prying eyes of police and informers and access to reliable receivers of highly valuable stolen property. These expert shop thieves play for high stakes. Every link in their chain of operation must be strong.

First, the shop-lifter and his helpers (who may number two or three) carefully consider which store to rob. This may take several days of observation and assessment of the stock displayed. Partners in the group take turns in visiting the shop to study the construction of the counters and to watch the habits of the staff. When they are ready to go to work, the group have worked out their plan of operation to perfection. They know the number of assistants in the shop, the busiest trading period, who is likely to be on duty at any hour of the day and all the details of the lighting and arrangement of the windows. They know, for instance, that assistant A has a habit of failing to close the shutter at the back of the window properly if he is asked to bring stock from it to show a customer. They know that assistant B, who shuts the window with care, rather fancies his ability to serve two customers at once. This slight conceit of B's (a failing fairly common among shop assistants who take a pride in their work) makes him all the easier to deal with as far as shoplifting teams are concerned. Wherever possible they make sure that the two "customers" such a man is serving are both members of the same team.

Not everyone has the right manner for buying diamonds of value, but the professional shop-lifters approach their victims with the casual indifference of the rich to whom the purchase of a stone worth a thousand or so is of no more consequence than buying a tie.

The first man in the team asks to see some of the store's best stones. While he and the assistant are busily examining and discussing the merits of a tray of diamonds, the second man enters the shop. Often he is accompanied by a woman, and the more attractive she is the better. They ask to see some item of jewellery in the window and, as the assistant gets it, each of the team can observe once again exactly how the assistant moves, how the sliding panel or door into the back of the window operates and whether it is firmly closed or not when the salesman returns to them at the counter.

Now the first customer makes it clear that he is impatient about being left alone. The salesman excuses himself from the second pair and hurries back to the man at the diamond tray. "This is hardly the sort of thing I'm looking for," says the diamond buyer curtly. "Have you nothing better?" The salesman must now turn away from both his prospective sales for a moment to fetch another tray of stones. He is uneasy about this, for jewellers are trained to be careful in such situations. He does not want to offend his diamond purchase, who appears to be a man of considerable means, by taking the first tray of diamonds off the counter. On the other hand he has three people in the shop and a great deal of valuable stock is exposed. The diamond buyer seems to sense the man's difficulty. "Here," he says, picking up the tray and handing it to the assistant, "You had better put these back first." As the salesman reaches for the tray it slips and almost falls to the floor. But the buyer, with superb timing, retrieves the tray just in time and only one or two stones roll to the floor behind the counter. This fumbling movement must be practiced assiduously for it to appear natural, but to an expert shop-lifter it is just the simplest of opening moves in starting the combined action which now takes place.

The salesman dives to retrieve the fallen diamonds, the buyer exclaims with annoyance and the man near the window coolly opens the back of the window and takes out the articles he has been planning to take for days. Even in the second or so that the salesman is retrieving the dropped stones, the theft is accomplished. By the time the victim has straightened himself up, soothed the irate diamond buyer (who complains at the man's clumsiness) the man near the window is calling for attention. He has decided to buy the cigarette case, but he would like it engraved. The diamond buyer can contain his anger at these interruptions no longer and, picking up his gloves and stick, he leaves the shop, to enter his car which is parked outside the doorway.

The man who has rifled the window completes his instructions concerning the engraving and says he will call back for the case the next day. He pays for it and leaves without any appearance of hurry. It may be several minutes before the salesman, upset by his unhappy experience with the diamond buyer who refused to wait, comes to place another cigarette case in the window—and discovers something is missing. The alarm is raised but the thief is already speeding away from the scene in the diamond buyer's car and calculating just how much they may hope to realize on the stolen goods.

In many cases, of course, the assistant may not notice there is anything missing from the window until he comes to clear it at the end of the day. By this time the thieves might well be in another country, or at least travelling by train or plane towards a new city and further raids.

One of the best window thieves was a man known to the underworld as The Goose, a Frenchman who worked with great success in England and was never caught on the job. He used to team with an accomplice called Stephen. The Goose posed as a gallant man of affairs whose act of choosing some pleasant trinket for a lady friend was a masterpiece of deception. He took infinite pains to seek the design that would exactly express what he called "the mood" of his gift and he was always on the point of being delighted with what he saw, yet just a little disappointed. Seeing that he considered only the most exquisite jewellery and was obviously a man to whom expense mattered little, salesmen were always anxious to please him and always very patient. He had good taste and charming manners and, although he was demanding, he was diffident about causing the assistant any trouble. His other attributes, less appreciated when his thefts were discovered, were the coolest nerve and the deftest hands in the business. They moved unerringly in a window although all he had to guide him were his delicate sense of touch and a remarkable memory which photographed the exact position of almost every item displayed. If he could get his hand into a shop window for two or three seconds he could remove just what he wanted without a mistake. He nearly always chose a shop which had heavy curtains at the back of the windows and not panels or doors. His partner created the diversion by pretended clumsiness or an arrogance of manner that was designed to fluster and annoy the staff.

The Goose was caught eventually and imprisoned for five years. But his downfall was not caused by any fault in his technique. He was foolish enough to quarrel with a receiver over the price of a haul and the receiver betrayed The Goose to the police. Receivers are always likely to be unreliable from the shop-lifter's point of view. Many receivers are in league with police and give thieves away when it suits them. This constant possibility of betrayal is one of the receiver's most powerful weapons in dealings with the underworld. It aids his bargaining when the seller of stolen gems knows that any serious disagreement over price may lead the receiver into becoming an informer. There are other advantages in this one-sided situation for the receiver. An occasional tip-off to the police enhances his reputation as a lawful citizen and it strengthens his control of his underworld contacts who cannot live without him, although they may distrust him deeply. The receiver, to the underworld, is a necessary evil. But, although he holds the whip hand most of the time, he is always a possible victim for a desperate criminal with a grudge.

One of the simplest shop-lifting tricks was used for many years by a suave and cunning Italian who was known throughout the underworld's diamond-stealing circles as Manuelko. He operated with his wife and, until he lost his nerve with the approach of old age, he was famous for his chewing gum technique.

Manuelko would enter a diamond dealer's premises alone, ask to see some valuable stones and then, as he waited at one of the small tables where such deals are carried out in many Continental establishments, he would slip a wad of gum under the edge or the inside surface of one of the legs. After much fussy examination and pondering, he would announce that there was nothing he wished to buy. But, at this stage of the operation, he would have already pressed one of the larger stones into the chewing gum. The hidden stone, of course, was suddenly missed and an inquiry would begin immediately.

Manuelko appeared as distressed as the dealer and his assistants. He would leap to his feet, stamp each leg and slap his clothes to see if the stone, by some strange chance, had fallen into some crease in his clothing. The assistants would search the floor, check the tray and look on Manuelko with growing suspicion. Then he would allow them to search him, his outraged protests growing stronger as their examination of his clothing and person proceeded. Eventually the dealer would have no choice but to let him go and to apologize profoundly for having inconvenienced him. A little later Manuelko's wife would visit the shop, ask to see some jewellery and quietly remove the hidden gem from its chewing gum cache.

Manuelko pulled this trick four times in a week in Rome when he was at the height of his career and then moved away to try it successfully in other cities both in Europe and South America. The gum trick was just one of Manuelko's repertoire of cunning methods and its greatest value, to him, was its almost childish simplicity.

Manuelko's chewing gum technique was the basis for another criminal's success in relieving stores of their diamonds. This man was operating in London with only a moderate amount of success in less exalted fields of pickpocketing when he heard of Manuelko.

He immediately improved upon the theme by the simple expedient of having an umbrella swinging on his arm as he entered the shop. He was well-dressed and, so it would seem to the shopkeepers, a man of means.

He asked to see a loose diamond, making the usual polite remark that accompanies such requests. While he was examining the diamond an accomplice walked in, distracted the attention of the employee and the thief slipped his diamond into a hole in the point of his umbrella where it rested snugly in the sticky embrace of a piece of chewing gum.

The assistant, having brushed off the annoying second visitor, looked puzzled when the criminal remarked boldly: "No, it's not quite the thing I was looking for," and prepared to walk out of the shop.

"But, sir, excuse me, I believe I left the diamond with you?"

"You did no such thing," replied the thief. "I remember handing it back to you just before that gentleman came into the shop."

The employee's puzzlement turned to alarm and a search began. No diamond. The thief, loudly asserting his rights as a customer and a gentleman, grudgingly submitted to a personal search of his clothing.

Even the folds of the umbrella were shaken. And when it was over he departed with the diamond still in possession stuck to the gum. For obvious reasons, this sort of deception could not be worked too often in the same city.

The improvement over Manuelko's system lay, of course, in the fact that the London thief did not have to wait until his wife or some other accomplice visited the shop to get the diamond. He simply walked out with it in a profitable effort at bare-faced daylight robbery.

On the two occasions that he employed his umbrella and gum in London stores he netted something over £12,000.

The underworld's expert shoplifters specialize in the theft of furs and the more expensive suiting materials. Sometimes they operate alone, but more often as a partnership. The women wear specially designed skirts with false fronts under which they can secret a remarkable volume of stolen materials. Some, in the fur coat business in New York have a trick of holding the stolen coat between their thighs while they make their exit from the shop. Women shoplifters are nearly always of middle age or older and, although their appearance is that of dignified matrons, their swift movements when they conceal a coat or a length of material are deft and supple enough.

The men work with an overcoat carried over one arm to cover the loot; sometimes they wear their coats and have hooks or big pockets in the linings to hold the stolen goods while they escape. One gang of London shoplifters stole several thousands of pounds' worth of furs at a big sale, making several visits to the crowded store and unloading each lot of loot outside into a waiting van. Furs, of course, are the ideal take for professionals who can sell them to receivers specializing in this type of merchandise. The stolen furs are cut up and re-made to avoid having them traced.

A lesser-breed of criminal, a sort of half cousin to the pickpocket, the shoplifter and the confidence man, is the short money-changer. His stock in trade is a brazen ability to claim that he has been short-changed and his skill consists solely in timing his requests for his exchange of large denomination notes for smaller ones. On the rare occasions when the short-change expert finds he has under-estimated his victim and a serious row appears to be developing he will suddenly find the disputed notes on the floor, apologize profusely and retreat to try his hand elsewhere.

The short-changers work on the principle of "little and often". They have only to succeed in cheating a shop or a bank or a restaurant of a couple of pounds seven times a day to achieve a modest living. It is generally a profitable sideline to other crime, or a handy emergency measure to gain ready cash while waiting for bigger jobs. The short-changers palm a note or two as their money is counted out to them, hustle the victim a little and impress them with an appearance of dignity and affluence so that the victim is hesitant about arguing too persistently when the crook claims his extra tribute. To hear short-changers talk one would wonder why anyone bothers to work honestly for a living. Their confidence in their own guile and their firm belief that the majority of people are fools is unhappily confirmed hundreds of times a day throughout the world.

Pickpocketing is perhaps as old as the oldest profession of all, prostitution. But it does not lend itself to organization on the same scale and the members of the trade are always limited in number to those who are prepared to acquire a special manual skill and combine it with expert and practical psychology. Nimble fingers, an ability to lie with conviction and a shrewd sense of which victims to select make up the basic requirements for success in this large group of individual performers in the underworld's ceaseless preying on honest men and women.

4

"the mafia"

ONE of the most interesting groups within the underworld in recent years has been the Mafia, the Italian secret society of crime which began as a sort of peasant's revolt in Sicily more than one hundred years ago and has now spread its methods of terror and extortion all over the western world. The underground exploits the normal world, but the Mafia exploits the underworld as well. The growth of this movement has been written about in a loose and general sort of way on many occasions, but few people realize how the Mafia operates, what its pattern of control has become or how powerful an influence it is.

The only way to achieve any real understanding of the Mafia is to first trace its beginnings. This takes us back to the Sicily of 1830, when the island that lies at the toe of the boot of the Italian mainland was so disorganized by wars and poverty that it was little more than an anarchy of peasant bandits.

For generations the Sicilians had been dominated and exploited by foreign powers and the young people were reared in an atmosphere of hatred and contempt for the police forces from the mainland. It is not only recent wars which have created the problem of juvenile delinquency.

Italy, devastated by the Napoleonic invasion of 1800, produced a series of minor leaders who ruled by force and fear and their agents crushed Sicily into a state of subjection. Later came the Italian struggle for liberation from the Austrian yoke and again war and disorder maintained the state of ruthless exploitation by officials and military opportunists. But the Sicilians were a hardy peasant race and their resistance to corrupt and violent rule, particularly that inflicted on them by the decadent Bourbon kings of Naples, took the form of fierce opposition.

By the middle of the nineteenth century, the bandit and robber gangs which had formed to strike back at foreign masters were in state-control. The island existed in a state of primitive anarchy with ruthless peasant gang leaders roaming the land to pillage and rob where they willed.

The land-owners knew no security unless they could organize their own defences. To do this they hired bands of armed retainers and turned them loose on the bandits. But these guards, men of the same sort and calibre as the bandits, soon changed their role as custodians of the landed estates. They discovered they could exist by extorting tribute from the peasants whether they were bandits or not. It was not long before these legalized groups of thugs became a law unto themselves and the Mafia, a series of loosely connected bands all engaged in what is now known as the "protection" racket, was born.

The origin of the name is obscure, but one likely theory is that the word Mafia is made up of the initial leters of the Sicilian words of a slogan created in 1860 by one of the most powerful gang leaders, Joseph Mazzini. Mazzini's slogan was, translated into English, "Mazzini authorizes theft, arson, poisoning".

This, in essence, has been the mainspring of power for the Mafia ever since. From this savage pattern of success based on fear, the society of the Black Hand (as the Mafia is often called) has built up a network of branches throughout the world.

The early Mafia bands operated a simple system. Land-owners who refused to buy them off would find their cattle stolen, their haystacks burned and their crops destroyed. If a landowner resisted these moves, his house would burn and, if he still showed fight, he would be killed. The power of the Mafia increased until it reached into the towns and cities. Soon, the dragnet of fear made it impossible for crops to be sold, or any business to be carried out, without some of the proceeds going to the society's agents. It was not long before the Mafia had a stranglehold on all business on the island.

It began as nothing but blatant blackmail, but it grew to be a form of "insurance". If a man paid the levies demanded of him, he would be assured of protection from thieves or assault by the society's thugs.

The Mafia, then as it is now, was not a single organization. It was a series of small bands. Often they fought bitterly over the loot, but they were united in their general principle of bleeding the middle class and wealthy.

The Mafia's complete ruthlessness was the secret of their success. They would kill, torture and rob with merciless efficiency. Men, women and children were all victims as the occasion suited. The men were often tortured and mutilated before they died, the women were raped, and kidnapped children were slaughtered as callously as a normal peasant would butcher a sheep or a goat. This ruthlessness, it may be noted, is reflected these days in the callous brutality of extortion mobs in America, South America and other countries where Italian and Sicilian migrants have transplanted and adapted Mafia traditions to modern living. How this happened, will be outlined later.

Eighty years ago in Sicily, rich and poor alike paid tribute to the Mafia bands. It was a straightforward system. Death was the penalty for those who refused to co-operate. The village milkman was the favourite agent. He would deliver a note asking for a certain sum when he called to milk his goats. This levy became known as "a little flower for the Mafia" and non-payment brought thefts, assault and sometimes death.

As the Mafia progressed they moved in on the wealthy city merchants by planting agents in almost every household and hotel to discover indiscretions in high places. Once information of this sort was gathered, the victim paid to keep the Mafia silent or they would ruin him. People who had property stolen could get it back by paying one-third of its value. It was much cheaper to cut losses this way than to go to the subdued and terrified police.

Only World War I interrupted this solid pattern of extortion on the island. Thousands of young Sicilians went to fight for Italy and came back determined not to submit to the Mafia's rule of fear any longer. Others came back determined to take over control of the network from their elders and bitter struggles began between the three factions—the old gangs, the reformers and the younger Mafia generation who were ambitious for power. For the ordinary people life became even worse than it was before the Mafia split; now the robberies and killings were more numerous than before as rival gangs exacted double tribute and carried on a war with the reformers at the same time.

It was not until 1924, when Mussolini visited the island and vowed to end the rule of the Mafia, that there seemed to be any hope for the oppressed. Extinction of the Mafia was one of the few promises that Mussolini made and kept—apart from making Italy's trains run on time. In a famous Palermo pronouncement, Mussolini said: "Five million patriotic Sicilians shall no longer be oppressed, put to tribute, robbed and dishonoured by a few hundred criminals." Mussolini appointed a high police officer, Cesare Mori, to clean the Mafia out.

It was a tough assignment. Sicily's strongest tradition was one of opposition to the police. Every Sicilian boy grew up believing that the only worthwhile role for a man was to become a "latitanza"—a criminal wanted by the authorities and living the life of a bandit on the run. This general admiration for the "badman", was reinforced by the attitude of the general population who sheltered and aided any man in trouble with the police. Generations of experience had taught them that this was the only way they could stay out of trouble themselves.

Cesare Mori, Mussolini's agent, was incorruptible and courageous. His first arrests included fourteen millionaires and a Knight of Italy, Signor Cuccia. The Mafia's power, Mori knew, had its strength in the highest circles as well as among the wild peasant bandits. Immediately there were protests to Rome and attempts to claim that Mori was just another Mafia thug in the pay of the very people he had been sent to attack. Mussolini ignored all the complaints, told Mori to get on with the good work . . . and arrested several of the Sicilians who had informed against him.

Mori established his first headquarters in the Madonie, a range of hills to the east of Palermo and one of the strongest Mafia strongholds in Sicily. The Mafia boss in this area was Gaetano Ferrarello, a man whose prestige was so high among the local populace that they referred to him as the Prefect of Madonie. He led a group of about 150 bandits, all of them living in mountain fortresses and with special hide-outs in a little town called Gangi. Here the wealthiest of the Mafia bandits had large homes with underground passageways cut in the rock to give them a means of escape should they ever be cornered.

Early in 1926, only two years after Mussolini's promise to

crush the Mafia, Mori carried out his major coup. He sent his *carabinieri* into the foothills of the Madonie to round up the racketeers—and the Mafia members moved cheerfully into Gangi. They had been warned of the coming raid. But they had not been warned of Mori's plan to surround Gangi once all the bandits were conveniently hiding in the town.

Before the Mafia leaders could discover the trap, the *caribinieri* had sealed off the town and occupied all its surrounding farms and villages. Mori sent an ultimatum into Gangi by the town crier, advising the hidden men to give themselves up within twelve hours or take the consequences of a pitched battle. Without waiting for an answer, Mori carried out a shrewd tactical stroke—he ordered his men into Gangi market-place. There they seized the cattle the Mafia robbers had stolen and sold them at bargain prices while the angry bandits wondered what they should do. The locals were vastly amused. This ridicule of the feared bullies and thugs was a damaging blow; for the first time decent citizens came to believe that they could take sides against the Mafia and hope to win. All the hidden men surrendered without firing a shot.

But the victory at Gangi was not all. Mori, at the same time, went after another notorious bandit, the former shepherd Grisafi whose gang dominated Agrigento, the most Mafia-ridden province in all Sicily. Despite the sullen silence of the locals when asked about Grisafi's crimes, Mori scoured the countryside arresting every man suspected of Mafia activity.

The respectable peasants and townspeople in the area were delighted. After a time even the poorer people found they could dare to become allies of the police and the hunt for the criminals went on with gathering speed. At last Grisafi and a group of his leading robbers were cornered in a house in the hills and they, too, came out with their hands up in abject surrender.

After these two major raids in the hills, Mori began his clean-up in Palermo and other cities and suddenly a great change came over the people of Sicily. Victims who had suffered in silence for years, began to come forward with evidence and complaints. Truck-loads of prisoners began to stream into the prisons every day as whole gangs were arrested at a time.

Mori was ruthless. If a suspected man ran into hiding, he

would arrest the bandit's wife and family and hold them as hostages until the criminal gave himself up. Hundreds of peasants and tradespeople swore to uphold the victory over the Mafia. These events took place over the years 1925 and 1929 and the effect on crime statistics in Sicily was astounding. In Palermo alone the annual toll of murders dropped from 268 to two in the four years, and robberies dropped from 300 in 1925 to four in 1929.

The Mafia appeared to have been crushed completely—in Sicily. But among the hundreds of Mafia thugs punished were many who were deported. Some went to Tunisia, some to Brazil and other South American countries and the majority went to America. It is in these areas that the Mafia was born again to flourish in a new environment.

The old methods of ruthless extortion paid off even better in the new countries where the Italian communities were easier to bleed than the tough peasant stock of Sicily. Life in the New World had brought many of the Italian migrants prosperity and far softer living than they had ever known at home. It made them all the easier marks for the exiled Mafia bandits. Now they worked in the teeming Italian section of New York, the boom towns of Brazil and richer fields of Tunisia instead of the rugged hills of peasant Sicily.

To understand just how efficient the Mafia system of blackmail and terror is, it is as well to realize some of the powerful forces that bind the Mafia branches together wherever they operate. The Mafia has no secret signs, badges, initiation ceremonies, rules of admission or accepted leaders. It exists in loosely connected groups, but there is a hard core of tradition which welds the gangs together.

Once accepted into the Mafia, a member can never leave it until he dies. Betrayal means death to anyone, member or victim; and information to the police is the worst form of betrayal.

The prohibition era in America provided the migrant Mafia members with an ideal harvest and they rapidly branched out into the other underworld trades of kidnapping, rum-running, blackmailing and murder. The great gang rule years of the 1930's in the United States produced ample proof that the Mafia was not dead merely because it had been routed out of Sicily. Many of the mob murders that appalled Americans were the result of fights between Mafia factions, struggling for power and a monopoly grip on vice and crime.

Among Mafia members openly named as such in America were Joe (The Boss) Masseria—eventually slain by one of Lucky Luciano's gunmen in the New York struggle for Mafia leadership; Joe Adonis; Albert Anastasia and Frank Costello. All big names in U.S. Crime.

To-day the Mafia is held mainly responsible for the enormous traffic in narcotics which has wrecked the lives of sixty thousand Americans, and claims fresh victims every year. The American branches of the society conduct their own public relations programme which is, on the surface, devoted to raising relief funds for distressed Italian families in their homeland and to bring relatives of American-Italians from Italy.

How much of this public front is genuine and how much it is merely a cover for the smuggling of Italian Mafia members into the United States no one can be sure. But the Federal Narcotics Bureau has been complaining for years that Mafia groups run the biggest and richest drug trafficking ring in the western world. As long ago as 1947, anti-dope chief Henry Anslinger said the Mafia gangs were planning to set up new dope headquarters in Tampa, Florida. The drug-pedlars he alleged, had shifted there from New York following big police raids there in the Harlem area.

Despite this warning by a high police official of what was going on, the Mafia managed to go ahead with its plans and most successfully establish their deadly business in Tampa, a tobacco-handling centre. In 1951, four years after Anslinger forecast what the Mafia were up to in America, a Congressional Crime Committee, inquiring into the gangster system in the United States, discovered that what Anslinger had prophesied had become fact.

The Mafia mobsters were said to be terrorizing the rest of the underworld by sending professional assassins around the country to wipe out members of rival gangs. This was part of a campaign by the Mafia-dominated groups to seize a monopoly of not only drugs, but the gambling and prostitution rackets as well. The official committee found that thirty of America's fifty leading gangsters were Mafia members.

Crime investigators found that in Tampa, once a quiet town,

the local chief of police had fourteen unsolved murders on his books—all in the past two or three years. This pattern of murder and terror was no new thing to the American public. As long ago as 1899, New York was subject to a wave of bombing, murder and blackmail of greater ferocity than anything the country had known before. It was believed then to have started when a Mafia refugee from Sicily, Ignazio (*The Wolf*) Saietta arrived in New York after killing a man in his native island.

In 1913, more than 130 murders were blamed on Mafia terrorists fighting one of their private feuds over the pickings to be had from the city's illegal enterprises. Bombs rocked Italian tenements almost daily and threatening notes from Black Hand agents, promising death to police informers, were a commonplace. It took three years of fearless police work to stamp out the ruthless violence of Mafia.

It is one of the characteristics of Mafia organization that it does not operate where the police force is strong and the local populace is used to strict law and order. The Mafia members include all types of criminal from the callous killers to the shrewd and indirect planners, like Lucky Luciano, who always used others to carry out their violent schemes. In the late 'twenties and early 'thirties, Mafia members made fortunes out of bootlegging and then, drunk with riches and power, began quarrelling among themselves over the division of territories and rackets.

This culminated in a long and bitter "war" in which Luciano finally took over the Mafia leadership in New York, following the murder of the previous leader, Joe Masseria. Masseria was one of the older generation. The theory is that Luciano and his younger colleagues in crime wanted to be rid of the older men whose methods were out of date. They considered them incapable of exploiting the crime market along modern lines.

It was in this era of the early 'thirties, that American crime became organized into a vast syndicate, in which seven or eight leading gangs agreed to work together, or at least to stop warring on each other. Prostitution, gambling and extortion were shared on a business-like basis so that each organization could extract its huge tribute without having to waste any of its resources on defending its dirty gains.

Then, in 1936, Luciano was jailed for thirty years on charges of enforcing prostitution and, for a time, the gangs were in retreat. But now they are back in business as strongly as ever. Luciano, released from prison in 1946 after serving only ten years of his thirty years' sentence, was deported to Italy. Ever since, the drug traffic has grown larger in America. Federal criminal authorities claim Luciano is piping drugs into the United States from his headquarters in Naples, using the international Mafia network of thugs and dope-pedlars to carry on the traffic.

It is easy for the police to lay the blame for all uncontrolled crime at the door of the Mafia, but there is seldom any concrete proof or evidence available. This is largely explained, most authorities agree, by the desperate secrecy of all Mafia activity and their fanatical determination never to tell the police anything. The only clues the police have gathered on the Mafia come from an analysis of scattered statements of unimportant crooks, but the pattern is clear.

The only way a criminal can enter the Mafia is to first commit a serious crime, such as murder or dynamiting. Having thus proved his capacity for violence, the new recruit is assured of a good income and freedom from arrest as long as he never breaks the Mafia code of refusing to talk, even under torture.

Despite this open police description of Mafia methods, they have not been able to arrest any of the suspected leaders. Police must have witnesses before charges can be made to stick, and the gangsters refuse to testify against each other.

Although the American investigating committee called hundreds of known gangsters before them in the course of their inquiry, no arrests were made. None of the witnesses "put the finger on" another. The modern criminal is far shrewder than his earlier counterparts were in the days of prohibition.

These days they always have strong legal representation in the courts and their accounts and income tax returns are made out by professional accountants. The men at the top are business executives who use every process of the law to cover up their operations. At the same time they can use the most primitive and violent action to have their wishes carried out.

It is a combination of cunning and ruthlessness difficult to match with normal police work and legal trial. The American law, designed to protect the average citizen against oppression, is used most effectively by the Mafia criminals to protect themselves.

In their early days in America, the Mafia preyed mainly on their own countrymen. They built up rackets in olive oil, spaghetti and fish. Just before the war a Mafia gang leader controlled the entire fish marketing system on the eastern coast of America. If a fishmonger did not sell within the price limits fixed by the gang, his trucks were overturned, his shops wrecked and his life threatened. And every trader in the fish business, from trawler owner to carrier, paid a proportion of his takings to the agents of the Mafia.

Here was a repetition of the old days in Sicily when the bandit gangs dominated peasant life first and later moved into the cities to control every business transaction in the island.

It may seem hard to believe that similar bandit tactics can operate successfully in a modern society, but the power of the underworld should never be under-rated. And the Mafia, remember, is almost an underworld within the underworld when it comes to terrorism and extortion.

Throughout years of activity in politics, in the unions and among the criminal society of America, Mafia leaders have built up enormous power. Many a big bank or pay-roll robbery, carried out by ordinary criminals, produces revenue for the Mafia members. They just advise the thieves that, unless they hand over part of the proceeds, they will either be turned over to the police or murdered. The criminal world knows there is nothing to be done but pay up—or take the consequences. In most cases they pay up. When they do not the newspapers get the story of another gang killing and the police have another unsolved murder in their records.

One result of the American inquiry into gang-bosses and their rackets was that many of the suspects fled to Cuba. Mexico and South American countries. Another result was that several police officers in Tampa were forced to resign for having accepted bribes from the Mafia gangsters.

The historic traditions of conspiracy and assassination, which shaped the pattern of Mafia groups in Sicily 100 years ago, have not weakened. Wherever the Mafia exiles have settled—in

America, in Tunisia and French North Africa—the old practices of blackmail and violence have flourished.

In South America a number of branches were established and the Buenos Aires group developed into a big organization with almost a monopoly in the prostitution field. But this hold was broken when brothels were abolished by the Argentine government and the Mafia members moved to Brazil. It is in the mushrooming city of Sao Paulo, where modern skyscrapers and two million citizens prosper at the heart of the great coffee-growing industry, that the Mafia now has its strongest hold.

Many of the senior police in Sao Paulo are Italian, or of Italian descent, and influence with the police is vital to large-scale racketeering. The Mafia is believed to have a big hold over gambling in Brazil, particularly over the running of the national pastime of *Bishos*, a betting game based on the winning numbers of the daily lottery. The returns from this enterprise in which millions of cruzeiros are invested by gambling Brazilians, are enormous.

The whole scheme is operated as a vast and highly efficient business. Thousands of Bishos shops trade on the street corners, hundreds of agents collect the takings and an army of clerks account for the income. But the directors, the brains behind the organization, control the whole illegal undertaking without taking part in it at all—except to exact their tribute. For "protection" against police action (an immunity which is assured by buying off the police) the Mafia gather in a large percentage of the proceeds, but there is still a big margin of profit for the Bishos dealers. It is the public who pays, as always, in the final analysis.

The Mafia system of collecting tribute is not confined to illegal businesses. It is simple enough for a criminal society like the Mafia, operating within the underworld, to learn about robberies, frauds, and other illegal gains.

The underworld pattern of personal contacts among various branches of criminals—a system maintained by a constant flow of gossip—is ideal for the Mafia. Their agents are everywhere and always alert for new opportunities. But the Black Hand can make itself felt in even the most reputable offices of importers and exporters once a gang decides a firm is making enough money to be able to spare a little. The Mafia picks its victims with great cunning and exploits only those who are likely to put up with blackmail for the sake of being unmolested.

A New York dealer in diamonds, for instance, was summoned by telephone to meet "a friend" recently. It was a stranger who spoke to him on the telephone, but it was explained that the suggested appointment "better be kept".

When the dealer met "the friend" in a cafe he found himself talking to a man who knew all about the diamond business and his own transactions in particular. It was explained that, in future, 30 per cent of his turnover would be paid to the Mafia. The alternative would be to leave the city.

The dealer refused. A week later a gunman shot him as he was entering his office in a big city building, but he was not badly wounded. In hospital the next day he received a note, unsigned, which said that next time Mafia's aim would be better. The diamond dealer closed his business down and moved his headquarters to Montreal.

To the police, the dealer was able to say only that an unknown man had threatened him, that a stranger had shot at him and that he could not understand why he should be so persecuted. The police reaction was that this perfectly legitimate business-man must have something to hide or, otherwise, the gang would not have bothered him. In the eyes of the law, the victim himself became suspect as a Mafia agent for the very simple reason that he "would not talk". For the Mafia, once they have established their organization, the system is fool-proof.

The traditional headquarters of the Mafia over the past century has been at Palermo, in Sicily, and the leadership of the movement in the island of its origin has always been a matter of deepest secrecy. The present chief of this strange secret society is known only to a few of the more senior members, but the former boss was Calogero Vizzini who died in 1953 at Villalba, the sulphur-mining town near Palermo. He was 77 and a dignified, white-haired man who could have been a provincial bank manager from his appearance.

He was given a most elaborate funeral with six black horses, bedecked with black ostrich plumes to pull his carriage. Hundreds of local peasants gathered to pay him homage as he lay in state in a room hung with rich tapestries for several days before he was buried. The Mafia's new leader is rumoured to be another Sicilian, Don Beppe Russo, but some observers claim Luciano may take his place.

This sort of doubt merely emphasizes how successfully the Mafia and all its branches have shrouded themselves with secrecy. Even the details of the connection between the Mafia groups in America and other countries and the senior, central group in Sicily has never been clarified.

But the loose and flexible pattern of Mafia crime that embraces the gunmen of New York, the gambling bosses of Brazil and the apparently respectable elders of Palermo certainly exists as an international clearing house of crime. The Mafia is a vast criminal club whose activities are betrayed only by the methods of violence and blackmail which are Mafia trade marks in whatever corner of the world it chooses to operate.

5

interpol

THERE is no greater proof of the enormous spread of organized crime throughout the world than the existence, since 1933, of Interpol—the International Criminal Police Commission. Interpol is recognized by the underworld as the longest arm of the law. More than fifty countries now belong to the Interpol network and its operations are greatly feared by the professional criminals. Once a man is listed by Interpol no port, airport or railway terminal is safe, the police of fifty nations can be alerted within hours to watch for any known criminal or suspect.

The underworld, of course, has its own methods of foiling Interpol but, despite the forging of passports and other documents of identity, the changing of names and appearance and the constant movement of crooks from country to country, Interpol methods are making international crime increasingly difficult.

Interpol (which is the telegraphic address of the I.C.P.C.) has its headquarters in Paris in the solid and respectable district of St. Cyr. There, in what appears to be just another Government building, labelled "Ministère de l'Intérieur," is an office into which flows, every day, a stream of information from all over the world. A Mexican bank-robber has been seen stepping out of a plane in New York; a Turkish confidence man disembarks from the overnight boat from Calais to Dover; a killer on the run from France is seen in a Rome cafe . . . these and thousands of other items of information like them set the Interpol network in action at any hour of the day or night.

The public hears little of Interpol's work. It is not a police force itself, merely an agency which collects clues to establish identity at a few hours notice and instructs the police on the spot to move. Thieves, counterfeiters, confidence men, dope-runners, smugglers, murderers and political refugees all come into the Interpol web from time to time. And every time a wanted man does come into the focus of the Interpol spotlight, its beam can probe any dive from Algiers to Alabama, or from Melbourne to Madrid.

This immense searching apparatus is able to work so efficiently because, in each country, the best brains in crime detection are enlisted to seek out and apprehend the wanted man. This book is designed to report on the working of crime from the underworld point of view. It is not by any means devoted to the detection of crime generally. But Interpol is such an important organization and so many of its methods are like the international techniques of criminal organization themselves, that it is considered essential to give some picture of its operation.

The underworld system of communications is based, as has been pointed out, on the continuous flow of secret information that flows among its members. Counterfeiters, smugglers and confidence men always know just where to go in any city of the world to check up on local conditions and to gather and exchange news of what is happening elsewhere.

Their sources of information are limitless and infinitely varied. Tips come from chamber-maids and corporation presidents, from street-cleaners and Senators. Wherever a crook seeks information he has ways of getting it.

The same sort of dark tide of information, given in secrecy, flows towards the police all over the world. Wherever there are criminals, there are informers. There is no honour among thieves. Criminal violence and extortion always breeds hatred and the desire for revenge. There is no easier revenge for the humiliated crook or the swindled racketeer than to tip off the police.

Much is heard about the stubborn refusal of criminals to talk to the police and it is true that the majority of hardened law-breakers refuse to co-operate in any way with the law. But what the public does not hear about is the information that police *do* receive. It suits the police not to reveal their sources of information. It also suits them to build up the picture of a universal criminal silence in the public mind.

The greater the general belief that crooks never tell the police anything, the greater protection does this give the informers whose identity is kept secret wherever possible to protect them from reprisals.

The vast underground community of sly informants that feeds information to the police of the world is invaluable to Interpol. At least, Interpol has made this huge mass of information valuable. In the old days local police knew plenty about the criminals within their jurisdiction, but they seldom knew anything of new arrivals until they discovered they had been at work. When a well-known suspect left a country it was no one's responsibility to warn other nations of the crook's departure.

Interpol has changed all this. The dossiers at the central office of the network contain over 60,000 names of known criminals, thousands of photographs and fingerprint records and intricate cross-reference filing systems for aliases and the alphabetical and phonetic spelling of names.

Perhaps a typical example of a recent Interpol case, as reported in *International Criminal Police Review* (the official organ of Interpol), will best illustrate both the complication of tracing crime and the international flavour of the underworld's "aristocracy" of forgers and swindlers. The names in this case are fictitious because Interpol never lets the world know what it is doing. Secrecy is its main strength, just as secrecy is the most vital element in all underworld operations.

On the evening of January 16th, 1955, a foreign sailor entered an inn in Kiel, Germany. He paid his bill with three counterfeit American Express travellers' cheques of twenty dollars each.

On being informed, the German police started investigations and contacted Interpol. (Here, immediately, is the immense difference between having international co-operation among police forces in the modern way, instead of the isolated efforts of local police confronted with denials, aliases and lies).

Kiel police airmailed a photograph of the sailor and a set of his fingerprints to Paris and, within ten days, they knew the true identity of their sailor. In the meantime, he having pleaded that the counterfeit notes had come into his possession innocently, the Kiel police had been obliged to release him. But they knew what ship he sailed in and that it would next call in at Liverpool on February 4th.

The sailor's real identity, Interpol reported, was one Veica, a Rumanian distributor of forged currencies and documents. With this already established by the time the Liverpool police picked him up, Veica was also identified by the hotel-keeper from Kiel.

Interpol's information on Veica, which had established him as an international counterfeiter's agent, made it worth while for the German police to fly the inn-keeper to Liverpool. Without this background on the suspect, no local police force in the world would have gone to so much trouble and expense to secure a conviction against an otherwise unknown sailor in the possession of forged money or cheques. Even if the amount had been a large one, the Kiel police might have taken months to discover the true identity of their man; they would have had to circulate his description to dozens of European police headquarters and, even then, been lucky to discover through his screen of aliases and denials that he was a notorious passer of counterfeit money. But in the files of Interpol all this had been checked and ferreted out in a few days.

Veica, confronted with police charges as to his true name and record, and freshly identified by the Kiel inn-keeper as the self-same sailor who had tried to pass three twenty dollar travellers' cheques about two weeks before, admitted he had been given the forged cheques by a Maltese called Soliano, who lived in London.

London police knew a lot about Soliano, but they had had no cause to interfere with his apparently legitimate business as a small shopkeeper in Soho in recent years. Now, on the basis of "information received" in Liverpool from a Rumanian crook and a Kiel hotel-keeper, the London police had good cause to search Soliano's premises. They found ninety-six other counterfeit travellers' cheques.

Soliano and Veica were both put under arrest immediately and on March 2nd the Old Bailey sentenced the two men to two years gaol for uttering and being in possession of counterfeit cheques. It took Kiel, Liverpool and London police—and Interpol—less than two months to secure a conviction against these men. In the old days even Veica's identity might not have been established in that time, without great persistence and remarkable luck. And if it had been established, the arrest of his collaborator could hardly have been achieved on the statements of a sailor in Kiel.

Before 1933, when Interpol was founded in the form of an

international flying squad of police drawn from five countries—England, Belgium, Holland, France and Germany—police had little or no means of co-ordinating their information and strength. In those days forged passports were far easier to obtain than they are now and, once a criminal left one country for another, he was almost untraceable.

It was a senior Scotland Yard official who made the first move to establish an international police system and he knew the size of the problem he was setting out to tackle.

"International crooks work on very skilled lines and are highly organized. It takes highly skilled police officers to defeat them," he said in his initial recommendation. "International thieves, confidence tricksters and forgers can be handled only by highly specialized officers with a thorough and detailed inside knowledge of their methods. It would be necessary to change the members of the squad frequently to prevent recognition by the gangs operating in these fields."

"If police officers could be given facilities to cross frontiers without formalities life would become much more difficult for the international racketeers." These original outlines for the system that was to become Interpol were nothing more than a beginning, but the qualifications of some of Interpol's recent and current officers show how other countries have co-operated in the building of the international team of experts to wage the fight against international crime.

One was the Swiss detective Werner Muller, an expert in the frontier-hopping tricks used by spies, confidence men and fugitives from justice in a dozen European countries. Swedish ballistics expert Harry Soderman studied criminal methods in Europe, America and the Middle East before he joined Interpol headquarters. From the Riviera, the haven of the confidence men, gamblers and counterfeiters from all over the world, came Monsieur Ducloux, a French sleuth with a knowledge of the luxury coast from Marseilles to Monte Carlo and a fabulous memory for faces. The Belgian psychologist and crime expert Monsieur F. E. Louwage revealed a deep understanding of human nature with his advice to the police of the world to "watch for the coquetry of women and the weakness elderly people have for scandal".

Confidence in the international flying squad grew rapidly

and, as more and more countries discovered the importance of enlisting the aid of other police forces to fight exploitation by the highly specialized racketeers of the modern underworld, Interpol acquired its present name. In 1937 fifty detectives, all specialists in their own areas and various departments of crime, met in London. They came from thirty-four countries, which shows how wide the police net was spreading against the professional crooks and the international organization of crime. Conference president was Dr. Michael Skubl, commissioner of police in Vienna (where a huge international dossier of underworld personalities was built up). He addressed the delegates in four languages—English, French, German and Italian. Nearly all senior members of Interpol speak several languages as well as their own.

In 1955 a congress for the prevention of crime was held for the first time under the sponsorship of the United Nations. Hundreds of delegates attended it in Geneva and the basis of representation was much wider than at the Interpol conferences, held each year in various capital cities of Europe.

To the United Nations congress went three main types of delegate. First were the members officially appointed by their governments as experts in crime prevention, second were representatives of "specialized agencies" (anti-narcotics bureaux, international currency control experts, and so on) and, third, there were the delegates representing police forces, prison officials, legal experts from the various courts, scientists and any other individuals who had a special interest in any of the thousand and one aspects of crime prevention and the treatment of prisoners.

This broad international approach to the problem of modern crime is another proof of the seriousness of the underworld's influence in the everyday lives of people in all countries of the world.

Interpol, itself, is growing more powerful each year. Its activities were, of course, interrupted during the six years of war in Europe, but it was revived by a meeting of police chiefs from many countries in Brussels in 1946. The revived Interpol's first task was to establish again the dossier of thousands of international crooks which had been lost when the Nazis occupied Vienna, the pre-war headquarters of Interpol's intelligence records.

Gradually a new "register of crime" was gathered. It was unexpectedly enlarged when, in 1949, a large part of the records lost in Vienna were found in the bombed wreckage of a flat occupied by a former Gestapo agent in Berlin. From this, and the newly-acquired details which flowed into Interpol headquarters, the organization now has more than 60,000 cards indexed and, in 1953, a special "Black Book" of major criminals was compiled for distribution to all main police offices in Europe, the Middle East, South America and other countries which support the Interpol network.

The Black Book contained the names, addresses, descriptions, aliases and records of at least 200 men and 17 women criminals and swindlers. American crooks were most numerous on the list with a total of 70 names and Australia, with 20 candidates for notoriety, provided the second largest membership of this far from exclusive crime club. The Black Book was compiled mainly on British initiative as a help to keep known and suspected crooks out of England in Coronation year.

Within a week or so of its distribution, the Black Book contributed to the frustration of an international confidence man who set out from Lisbon to travel to London by air. A telegram to St. Cyr headquarters told Interpol the crook was on his way and, by the time he stepped from his plane at London airport, the police were waiting for him.

Scotland Yard's special branch detectives and immigration officials at all ports and points of entry to Britain had been alerted, just in case this professional swindler changed his travel plans after leaving Lisbon. The London detectives picked their man out of the passport queue and sent him back to Lisbon. About forty other international crime stars were halted as they arrived in Britain before the Coronation and politely sent back to the Continent because of Black Book information.

Police specialists from all over the world visit London, or attend the conventions held by Interpol to brush up on new methods and to improve their systems of co-operation with other police systems. Britain pays Interpol £1,000 a year to be a member and a special room at Scotland Yard is set aside for Interpol liaison work. Paris now has a special radio-transmission system, on a secret wavelength, which keeps all members of Interpol in constant and almost immediate contact.

The only way for the police to tackle the operation of air freight smugglers, currency and drug smugglers and airline thieves has been by radio-warning of the movements of the professional crooks in these highly organized fields. Although the American Federal Bureau of Investigation chief, J. Edgar Hoover, withdrew his organization from Interpol in 1950, this place in the detection network was filled by the U.S. Treasury department which, in the American scheme of administration, controls the Narcotics Bureau. This bureau, in turn, is linked with the Customs Bureau, and all U.S. operations against drug trafficking, counterfeiting, general smuggling and other major offences with international tie-ups are still aided by Interpol intelligence.

One of the most highly organized counterfeiting rings in the history of crime was broken a year or so after the war through co-operation between the American Treasury's detection agencies and Interpol. The currency forgers were distributing American dollars, a type of currency which is bought at a premium in almost every country of the world.

Information coming to the busy rooms in the Ministère de l'Intérieur building in St. Cyr indicated that the gang's headquarters were in Europe and the dollar-exchange markets of several countries were being flooded with counterfeit notes.

Seeing that so many dollar transactions were conducted outside the currency regulations it was difficult to track down the distribution of these worthless notes—nobody wished to inform the police of being cheated when his own part in the transaction was itself illegal. But, gradually, the scattered complaints and tips from informers in a dozen different capitals from New York to Rome were pieced together at the central clearing house of clues in Paris. Eventually, French detectives raided a lonely farmhouse in Normandy where they found a stack of forged American notes with a face value of 234 million dollars.

Within a year of this police victory, a secret Interpol plan to round up a group of air smugglers was carried out most successfully. The operators of this racket used a series of privately chartered planes to move the proceeds of hundreds of robberies of jewels, bonds and cash from Britain to Europe and the Middle East. A ring of receivers had organized this method of realizing on their huge stocks of stolen goods. By alerting police forces in more than twenty countries, Interpol was able to set up an international watch on the movements of all private aircraft and to link these movements with appearance of jewels and cash in the various black markets of Europe.

The principal problem still confronting Interpol is that of getting uniformity in the extradition laws and procedure between the more than fifty member countries. A convention to standardize these procedures is under discussion by United Nations authorities in this field.

Interpol, which is sponsoring this move, would like to have legal processes which would enable police in any member country to arrest wanted men and ship them back to wherever authorities are demanding their presence. But present laws governing this sort of action are full of discrepancies. All are based on the old ship and rail days of transport in which a few days delay in getting legal formalities straightened out did not matter particularly. But now, when a man can be in New York one day and Rome the next, old systems of arrest and extradition are hopelessly cumbersome.

This matter of quick seizure and extradition, however, must be carefully controlled. Interference by foreign police with the liberty of citizens away from their own countries is a breach of nationality rights most bitterly opposed. It must be remembered that before police may arrest an internationally wanted criminal they must make sure that the extradition of their suspect is, in fact, demanded by the legal authorities, as well as the police, of his own country.

The police seeking an arrest must also forward to the police who will apprehend the criminal complete particulars of an indictment. There have been, and still are, many cases in which an arrested man has been able to escape from the clutches of of the law because extradition procedure left him legal loopholes for insisting on his release.

One suggestion made to avoid this sort of embarrassment for the police whose countries are members of the Interpol system, is to make Interpol headquarters the central authority for all extradition requests. This would avoid all the time-consuming and sometimes involved procedure required now when, although a police force is ready and able to arrest a man, its hand may be stayed by the need for governmental permission to act—a permission not granted in most countries without elaborate documentary proof and legally attested statements to support the case.

Only last year the Secretary-General of Interpol, M. Marcel Sicot of the Sureté Nationale in Paris, was emphasizing the need for I.C.P.C. to have more clearly defined legal grounds for swift arrest and rights to extradite criminals to the country which requests them to face criminal charges. Before a clear-cut and decisive system can operate, the police systems of the world must carve their way through thick jungles of political conventions and constitutional treaties which most governments are reluctant to adjust.

Interpol does, however, achieve some remarkable feats of detection and police action. Their resources of information and watchfulness are never more sorely taxed than in the case of big drug-running organizations. These groups of underworld characters operate by such devious means, and their control is so cunningly hidden in a screen of agents, aliases and remote influences that it is possible to give an idea of the scope of Interpol action in such cases only by quoting an example.

Again, Interpol refuses to disclose the real names of the men involved, but the size and nature of the problems they tackle is graphically illustrated in the following account of how a group of drug-pedlars was smashed. The gang first established a business by sending drugs from Lebanon, Italy and France to the Arab markets in Egypt, Libya and Tripolitania. After operating for two years in these areas, the drug ring decided to extend its activities to America where, although the risks are enormous in sending shipments across the Atlantic, the rewards are just as great.

It was in 1953 that this dope-ring's traffic was first reported to the Rome branch of the United States' Narcotics Bureau. The Americans passed their information on to Interpol and the Italian police who succeeded in exposing the organization. The traffic was chiefly in raw opium, which was intended for the preparation of heroin in Italy, and hashish. The drug ring's code names for these commodities were "lienen" for hashish, "cotton" for raw opium, and "silk" for heroin.

The head of the organization, it was established, was a Lebanese called Mansour Kahat who lived in Beirut. He worked with another Lebanese, Bcharré, who lived in the same town. The most important go-between was a French subject, born in Cairo, who was known as El Faris. This man had the drugs smuggled into Italy with the aid of a man named Djemal, a sailor on board an Egyptian ship carrying tourists from the Middle East to Europe.

The police discovered the first shipments, crates of dates, first at Rome and then at Genoa. But these transactions would not have been tracked down had there not been trouble among some of the distributors over their being paid in counterfeit money. The vast profits they were making out of smuggling, it seems, were not enough for the ringleaders—they wanted to rob their fellow traffickers by paying them off in worthless notes.

El Faris's principal agent was an Italian, Marco, who had three Italian accomplices—Loria, Leone and Montini—and an Argentinian, Tosine.

Italian police, acting on their instructions, first relayed to Interpol for checking on the identities of the suspected men, were able to pick two of them up in Rome on June 15th, and the others in Genoa two days later. When they were arrested, these men had in their possession 54lb. of hashish; 2lb. of morphine; ½lb. of heroin; several boxes of dates, with double bottoms designed to secrete drugs; and items of drug-peddling equipment, such as fine balances, talcum powder (to break down the drug) and tins of condensed milk (another substance much favoured to dilute drugs before they are sold as "pure" to the hungry buyers).

The prices for the drugs then ruling (1953) in Europe were 25,000 lire a pound for hashish, 200,000 for morphine and 400,000 lire for heroin. The pedlars also had seven thousand dollars' worth of fake travellers' cheques which they planned to sell at about half the black-market rate of dollar currency. They also had 1½ million lire in legal currency.

Some of the forged travellers' cheques had been stolen, it was later established, from a Mexican tourist in Rome; others had been lifted by pickpockets in Rome buses. Here, in this one round-up of half-a-dozen crooks, was a combination of drug-running, forgery, theft and smuggling experts and considerable resources in legal money. Reports from Libya, through Interpol, showed El Faris was known there as a confidence man; from Paris came reports of El Faris having been about to open negotiations with an Italian drug ring in Harlem, New York—but these had fallen through when El Faris suspected he was being swindled.

The outcome of this operation was that El Faris, Marco, Loria and Djemal (the courier on the Egyptian ship) were gaoled on charges varying from receiving stolen property to smuggling, forgery and violations of the harmful drugs Act.

The principals, of course, were not uncovered. They, no doubt, are still operating with a ncw chain of command and a new team of distributors. But, without the swift intelligence system of Interpol, the gathering of information from American narcotics men in Rome and the co-operation of the Libyan police, none of the criminals might have been either arrested or punished.

Interpol's exchange of information is not limited merely to clues for the tracking down of crooks. It includes an international exchange of specialist instruction in crime detection, collection of evidence and practical advice from many specialists in the handling of criminals and the encouragement of informers among the underworld community. Interpol is also interested in other branches of international co-operation, such as the repatriation of children and the prevention and cure of social problems allied to crime all over the world.

Its strength is a living proof of the value of international co-operation and understanding in the universal battle against crime. Interpol is the exact opposite of the dreaded Mafia, both in its methods and its aims, but the underworld fears it more than the terrorist activities of the Black Hand gangs.

6

prostitution

PROSTITUTION, according to the dictionaries and the encyclopædias, is "promiscuity for gain". But these cold, dry words are nothing more than a bookish definition of the oldest profession in the world and the most shameful activity known to man. "Promiscuity for gain" covers a whole universe of lust that leads men and women to buy and sell flesh for the satisfaction of the most instinctive and primitive desire next to the desire to eat.

From the sweltering *Street of Cages* in the steamy back streets of Bombay (where a man can walk hundreds of yards past open-fronted, barred dwellings to take his pick of the sullen, waiting women) to the luxurious apartments of the high-priced "call-girls" in New York, the sordid, dirty trade is the same. And to the underworld, which knows almost nothing of love, these hardened, lost women provide almost the only sex life that male criminals ever experience. Most crooks, whatever branch of the underworld they inhabit, get involved in some way or another with prostitutes.

This is so in spite of the fact that the general run of crooks loathe and distrust pimps, panders and stand-over men. But brothels are an ideal hiding place for criminals, a lost world where they can wait between jobs away from, and yet close to, the normal life on which they prey. Brothels provide a place where they can mix freely with their kind and live their brutalized lives relatively free from police interference and the suspicious prying eyes of decent people.

Prostitution, it seems, has been an inevitable accompaniment of human society in the western world during the past 3,000 years. In ancient Greece the *dicteriades*, as the prostitutes were called, were registered, controlled by the police and had to wear distinctive clothing. The Romans were the first society to strongly disapprove of prostitution and women involved in the trade had to dye their hair yellow and be licensed. There were severe penalties for treating them with anything but the coldest cruelty and it was not until the later, and decadent years, of the Roman Empire that these women became so numerous and influential that all the old social barriers of loathing and isolation were broken down.

The early Christian attitude to prostitutes was one of charity, tolerance and even forgiveness and, with the age of chivalry, it was considered noble to rescue fallen women from their tragic plight. In the twelfth century, Pope Innocent III considered it a praiseworthy act for a man to marry a prostitute and reform her life.

In the Middle Ages brothels flourished all through Europe and "promiscuity for gain" attained what now seems a grotesque standing. Prostitutes were licensed and regulated and, in France, whole towns were turned into centres of prostitution. The ancient town of Toulouse, for instance, depended for its prosperity almost entirely on its bordello trade and the city and the university shared the profits!

Then came the Reformation and throughout the fifteenth and sixteenth centuries public opinion revolted against the tolerance of such breeding grounds of disease as lawful brothels. A campaign against prostitution spread through many countries. It had little effect. Prostitution remained as widespread as ever and its dangers increased.

The next development was to attempt some regulation of the trade again and the changes of policy that occurred throughout the eighteenth century were nothing more than various methods of police and state control procedures. Gradually, the general pattern of police responsibility for keeping an eye on the European brothels became the universal custom.

It was not until 1899, when the first congress to consider the evil of "white slaving" (the shipment of women from country to country) was held in London that the modern attitude to prostitution was first developed. This congress was followed in 1902 by a similar conference in Paris and the first international agreements to limit and discourage the export of girls to foreign countries was drawn up and signed.

Broadly speaking, there are two national attitudes to prostitution to-day—unofficial checks on the trade through police action (as in Britain and America); and tolerance of registered houses under police and medical supervision as in some European countries and in South American cities.

The history of prostitution in the East follows different lines, but there, where prostitution has often been connected in some measure with religious practice, the attitude is quite different to the overall European one of disapproval and furtive guilt.

The strongest link between the underworld criminal and prostitutes has always been the somewhat surprising fact that, for many whores, their greatest ambition is to marry a crook. Perhaps it is not so surprising. These women have no hope of marrying honest citizens and there is possibly a great deal of truth in the theory that a criminal (particularly a man who forces his woman to keep on working to provide him with easy money) is the only type of man who can give a prostitute a sense of superiority. It is hardly an ideal basis for love, as the normal person knows it, but it is all the underworld has in the way of gentler passion. There are, of course, other angles to these sordid relationships. Criminals get their money easily and when they have it they spend it extravagantly. They like to lavish gifts on their women—it is a means of building their own prestige.

In America, despite the big purge of brothel racketeers in the late 'thirties, the link between prostitution and crime is still very strong. After all, prostitution is a ten million dollar a year industry in the United States, according to some authorities, and this is far too great a traffic for gangsters to leave un-exploited. In South America the position is even worse.

American criminals, in the main, have no direct interest in brothels but derive their considerable income from them by extortion and "protection", but in South America many houses are actually owned and operated by crooks, who use the same premises as places of residence and hide-outs, or as a cover for their other rackets.

A recent survey of prostitution in America showed that prostitutes there are nearly all in the grip of the gang bosses through the system, established by the big crime syndicate that turned vice into big business twenty-five years ago, of providing medical supervision for the women working in brothels and arranging legal aid for them when they run foul of the law.

They put up bail, hire lawyers, pay fines for the "girls"—and then deduct all these costs plus a large commission from their later earnings.

There are also charges for rent, food and clothing, laundry and light accounts to be deducted from an operator's earnings, plus a commission for the madam, before the unfortunate woman concerned has any money for herself. It is no wonder that they seldom get out of debt or, if they do, that they have not the moral fibre to retire from the trade and attempt to set themselves up as normal citizens.

Perhaps one of the worst brothel areas in the western world to-day is Bon Retira area in Sao Paulo, Brazil. Here there is a whole street, several blocks long, entirely given over to brothels where women sit all day, in various states of undress, by open windows to entice customers from the roadway. There can be no greater instance of mass degradation anywhere. Sao Paulo, a rapidly growing city about 200 miles south of Rio de Janeiro, is 3,000ft. above sea level and has an ideal climate. There is a ten-minute air service from Rio to shuttle the tourists in and out, and the city of two million inhabitants is a centre for the Brazilian troops. Bon Retira contains more than one hundred brothels each with ten to fifteen girls, and the ruling price is fifteen cruziero, the equivalent of four shillings.

These are the dregs of humanity, the lowest grade in the profession. But there are hundreds of other more expensive girls to be bought, and it is almost the usual practice for well-to-do Brazilians to keep one or two girls. Most of the women are locally born these days, but before the war, the brothels were recruited from the Spanish, French, Rumanian, Polish and Hungarian immigrant prostitutes, whose journeying far from their own lands, in search of riches they could not hope to achieve at home, became known under the misleading title of "white slavery".

There have been international commissions on the "white slave traffic" and agreements to prohibit the travel of these women to foreign countries. Tighter control of all personal movement about the world has helped to limit the migration of prostitutes, but there is a misconception about the term "white slaving" which should be cleared up. The popular impression is that, somehow, evil men have tricked, lured or abducted thousands of innocent young girls into brothel slavery far from their native lands.

This story, to those who have observed the set-up in South America personally, is a weird distortion of the truth. The women who travel to Buenos Aires, Rio and other South American cities and become prostitutes there have seldom, if ever, made the journey without knowing exactly what they are doing, or what their lives would be like. Is it conceivable that hundreds of innocent women could be shanghaied, transported across the globe and forced to sell their bodies to all and sundry without being able to protest? Hardly. No, the women who have made these journeys have nearly always been prostitutes before they set out, or attached to criminals whose purpose in taking a woman with them to another country has been only too clear to both parties.

We shall discuss later the methods by which the brothels of the world are recruited, but it is well for the reader to understand that it is not by "white slavery" as it is popularly imagined. The "white slavery" theory always receives a prominent display in the popular and sensational Press of the world, where it makes ideal "copy" and conjures up horrible visions of abduction and callous cruelty. But the truth is not as exciting as that, although it is just as sordid.

One of the most easily traced patterns of the international hook-up in crime may be seen in the tradition among underworld travellers of always seeking out brothels when they reach a new city or town. Criminals have plenty of reasons for not wishing to expose themselves in ordinary hotels, particularly when they are likely to be a little conspicuous because of their strangeness in a new setting, and it is in brothels that they obtain much valuable information and contacts.

Big hotels have their own detectives and small hotels are highly suspicious of strangers. The police, in every city of the world, keep an eye on hotel guests and have their informers on the hotel staffs. Compared to the quiet, shadowy world of the brothels, even the average hotel is bathed in a glare of official inspection that is far too uncomfortable for the underworld peace of mind.

But accommodation in a brothel is a different proposition. Here the criminal can make immediate contact with the local crooks, learn all he needs to know about local conditions and relax, safe in the knowledge that any prying eyes will do no more than report his presence to other criminals—nearly all brothels must have police protection. Being a police pimp in these surroundings is too dangerous an occupation for even the most ardent informer although, of course, there are exceptions. But they are rare.

There are, in many cities, definite arrangements for the shelter and protection of visitors among the bordello-keepers and prostitutes generally; after all, a newcomer is always likely to be a good customer and both the stranger and his obliging hostesses benefit from their association.

The international name for such places of accommodation is *melinas* and regular travellers sometimes keep a stock of their tools of trade in several of these places to facilitate their operations as they move around on their circuits of crime. The criminal contacts to be made in *melinas* are inexhaustible. They vary from direct access to gang bosses to re-unions with old partners; from contact with the young element among the criminal rackets to the veterans, many of whom marry madams and settle down as proprietors so that they may live out their final years in comparative security and ease.

Prostitution, which has flourished all over the world ever since mankind began to live in large communities, is a perfect example of the way violent opposition to an evil forces it underground where it not only survives, but increases. It has been suggested that modern attitudes to sex with their greater tolerance of irregular relationships outside marriage might well deal prostitution a more severe blow than any attempts to prevent it by legislation. But there have been other trends to counteract this possible development.

Sexual licence is much more prevalent than it used to be fifty years ago when the only outlet men had for their sexual appetites outside marriage was to be found in prostitution. But there seems also to have been a general coarsening of behaviour, a far freer discussion of sex, and generally speaking, a far greater incitement to sexual activity in recent years. This latter trend, plus the fact that many men have been in the Services in recent years, has not only kept prostitution as busy a profession as it was in the days when conventional moral attitudes drove men to bought pleasures, but has even increased the traffic in hired bodies. It has also created what might be termed "a higher standard of prostitution".

An outstanding instance of how modern conditions have changed the prostitute's outlook on life may be had in the recent London case of the prostitute who wished to sue a newspaper for publishing her address when she was fined on a street-walking charge at Bow Street. The woman said she did not object to having her professional name published, as this is one of the hazards of her business, but she claimed the publication of her private address was a malicious libel and she called on her lawyer to see if she had a reasonable case.

What incensed her most was the fact that for years she had lived in a most respectable block of flats as a conventional, middle-class widow. She had a son at one of the better-known public schools and her whole life, as far as her prosperous neighbours knew, was beyond reproach.

"Now this has happened," she said, referring to the publication of her address, "I shall be forced to move and the effect it may have on my son may be disastrous."

"You do not deny that the charge against you was correct?" asked her lawyer.

"No. But surely that is my business. It has nothing to do with my private life," the woman said. "What I am objecting to is the quite unnecessary persecution this paper has committed in trying to destroy my private reputation."

"I have my professional rooms, near Piccadilly Circus. The paper could have printed that address and I would not complain. But this advertising of my private flat is malicious. Already my telephone has started to ring at all hours of the day and night and strange men are pestering me."

She was most indignant about this, as her normal clients were chosen only after careful consideration and strictly limited in number. As a prostitute of "some standing" her services were exclusive to a small list of customers, her discretion was always to be counted on and her whole mode of operation was on the expensive and specialized scale. She was well-dressed, well-spoken and a woman of considerable poise and charm. She had her son's name to protect as well as her own.

The lawyer considered her case and had to advise her that

she would not be likely to have any chance of success in a claim against the newspaper concerned. Her admission that she was a prostitute, no matter how exclusive, would bar her from any serious legal standing in a case for libel.

Surely such a situtation, a serious claim against a newspaper for defamation of character by a prostitute could never have occurred in the past! But one of the features of modern prostitution is the growth of a large class of discreet and apparently respectable women who earn good livings at the same trade as the abject and degraded creatures in Sao Paulo and the caged victims of lust in Bombay.

The civic authorities in the Middle Ages tried to seal brothels off from the rest of normal living in a vain bid to protect society against venereal diseases. The same attitude, refined only by the more intricate bureaucracy of modern states, persisted in Poland and other middle European countries until recent years. "Black" passports, V.D. clearance certificates, police supervision and registration and inspection of houses of prostitution—all of these devices to legitimately control the purveyors of lust have had as little success in reducing the incidence of the trade as the old isolation of brothel areas and the savage punishments of stoning to death, or public humiliation and flogging, did one thousand years ago.

This survey of prostitution is not designed to inspire moral indignation, but to outline the facts. They are far from pleasant, but an evil is never overcome by ignoring it or by hiding it from open view. Frank discussion, not on the basis of long-winded official reports or outraged opinion, but on the truth as it is discovered by an average man's experience and inquiry has seldom been attempted. Most men talk knowingly about prostitution because it is considered to be a subject that any red-blooded male must have at his command. But the "average man" is not the depraved and unhappy creature who finds his sexual satisfaction regularly among prostitutes. His experience is nearly always limited to sly and infrequent visits, generally in his blundering youthful experimental years. Like the rest of the underworld, the dark jungle of prostitution is almost entirely unknown to decent people to whom its customs and standards of behaviour are as foreign as the language and habits of the Martians.

Prostitutes—known as "grafters" in underworld terminology—may be classified into four main categories: ordinary brothel workers, who may satisfy as many as a hundred visitors every twenty-four hours; street walkers, whose privilege of selecting their clients goes hand-in-hand with other activities, such as theft and "standover" tricks; the call girl, who operates in the most exclusive circles at prices prohibitive except for the wealthiest patrons; and the hotel-bar and dance hall "pick-up", who is generally a call girl on her way down the scale and an expert in encouraging her customers to spend as much on drink (for which she gets a percentage on the sales) as on her own charms. And among them is the small but not insignificant number of prostitutes, both male and female, who cater for the perverted pleasures of their own sex.

The psychology of prostitution, a subject which has excited many otherwise dry-as-dust professors, is basically very simple. Poverty, lack of moral training, and coercion by pimps or brothel-keepers are the three main causes. The proportion of girls tricked, or sold into prostitution is very small, even allowing for the number of girls who are said by outside observers to have been made victims in this way.

What is just as interesting, but has received remarkably little attention from the experts, is the male attitude to purchased "love" with its inevitably sordid and often dangerous setting. The human male, of course, is basically a promiscuous creature, seeking his sexual satisfaction wherever he can find it. Man likes to think of himself as a hunter and to regard every sexual adventure as a conquest; to enjoy his encounters with women partly as demonstrations of his superior strength.

The romantic, maternal emotions play little part in the male role among primitive societies and modern man, tamed and confined in our intricate pattern of "civilized" living, no longer is allowed to wander at will among the community seizing his women wherever and whenever the spirit moves him.

For the great majority of men, so the experts are now discovering, normal marriage and a lifetime of faithfulness to one woman may be morally good, but it is a frustrating experience. The desire to express his old, primitive urges of mastery over women is always with him in some degree, no matter how well he may appear to have adapted himself to the conventions of polite society and the responsibilities of fatherhood and family life.

If a man does not find his marriage satisfactory in the sexual sense, the delights of illicit love, of casual lust with submissive women, become increasingly attractive. So he turns to prostitutes. With them there is no question of having to flatter a woman, to pay court, to undertake to care for her and be responsible for any outcome that their union may have. It is a carefree, strictly business contract whereby, in return for cash, the male can take his pleasure and depart. Just how many men succumb to this temptation is not known because it is a secret, furtive business. But the thriving trade of prostitution all over the world reflects the constant male demand for licentious women.

Men, who frequent brothels purely as customers and not as criminals, with no interest in them other than the satisfaction of their physical needs, often buy love for other reasons than sexual desires. They are not likely to admit any other reason for buying the prostitute's substitute for love, but modern psychology claims that such men, in many cases, want to assert themselves to impose their will on some other person.

They are also anxious, in many instances, to exercise a sense of possession and, although there is little satisfaction in "owning" a woman for a few minutes merely because she has been bought, it seems to satisfy the brothel patron. It is a cheap and sordid purchase to satisfy a primitive need, but one has only to see the queues of men that form outside the prostitution houses in any city near an army, navy or air force area in wartime, to realize what an urgent need it can become among men robbed of normal relations with women.

There are also many men, even in these enlightened days, who consider the sex act is an unclean and sinful business, something not to be enjoyed with the women they marry—at least not enjoyed in the primitive way they desire secretly and never care to admit in their own homes. To such men brothels are the only place where they can hope to achieve the satisfaction that is denied them through their contacts with decent women.

In the eyes of modern specialists, such men are immature personalities, men who have failed to grow up mentally. They have not reached the stage of emotional development where they can understand that satisfactory sexual love demands a contribution from both parties. Failing to make the necessary contribution themselves, they fail to arouse the necessary response from their wives. To overcome this lack, they seek to buy it. But a man cannot buy love: all he gets from a prostitute, even the most expensive and skilled of them, is release from a physical tension and desire that can never be anything more than a coarse imitation of the true spiritual rewards of love.

From the women's point of view, prostitution is an even greater tragedy, which brings the development of depraved appetites, and the constant burden of self-disgust which no amount of glittering jewellery and fine clothes can shed. It is no wonder that they seek oblivion and forgetfulness in alcohol, and sometimes drugs, as their debased lives drag through the years and their physical charms deteriorate.

It is poverty which drives most girls into prostitution; poverty of intellect as well as material poverty. In western countries, of course, it is not grinding poverty which reduces a girl to making a decision between getting enough to eat or surrendering her virtue. But the glitter of an easy life, the attraction of the much advertised gaiety of city amusements are enough to make the less intelligent girl convinced that the sale of her body can bring the happiness she desires.

It is this false goal which leads the great majority of women into prostitution, but there are many other factors. Unhappy homes, crowded living conditions and parental cruelty drive many girls into the arms of bad companions; there are always unscrupulous men ready to take advantage of the young girl's desire for admiration and love and then to discard her. It all sounds a little old-fashioned and "corny", but prostitutes are made, not born; and the making of them follows the old pattern once a girl abandons the hard path of virtue for easy living and base moral standards.

Prostitutes are being recruited all the time, everywhere, by the underworld's shabbiest characters—the pimps and stand-over men who prey on women for a living. Sometimes such men are married and fathers of families. By some weird division of their lives they can play two roles; one as an apparently normal citizen and the other as a parasite who bullies and hounds his unfortunate victims so that he can extort a tribute in money from their misfortune.

It was just such a man who finally broke down and, to protect his family from shame, decided to inform the New York vice squad of his part in the enormous pre-war brothel and prostitution racket. His name was Dave Miller and, in return for his information, he got police protection from the gangsters who controlled the racket and all charges against him as a procurer were forgotten. It was in this campaign against the underworld dope and brothel czar, Lucky Luciano, that dozens of underworld thugs were convicted and imprisoned and the horrifying network of extortion and vice was crippled; for the time. That was in 1936, but recent reports indicate that the prostitution business in New York is as prosperous and as busy as ever it was.

It is difficult for the ordinary man or woman to imagine how any man can prevail on his wife or girl friend to hire her body for his profit, but it happens all the time among underworld people. Their standards of morality allow this sort of behaviour without anyone even questioning its decency.

To most of the people within the prostitution business it is a trade the same as any other. A middle-aged pimp in Paris confided recently that he was unhappy, deeply depressed about his life.

This was such an unusual statement from a man of this type that he was asked to explain how he had come, after years of living on the sordid earnings of his wife and her sister (these were the women he "managed" and had exploited for some thirty years!) to view his life with distress and remorse.

"Oh," he said, "I am not worried about that. We have worked honestly enough, but Marie and her sister will no longer obey me. They are too old to knock about, you understand, and I no longer have any control over them. But they will insist on working still when we have no need to stay in business.

"We could have retired three years ago (Marie has always been a good manager of our finances), but she and her sister absolutely refuse. They have become greedy for money." He announced this with infinite regret.

"And I, who have been looking forward for years to setting

ourselves up out in the country to enjoy a little peace and quiet, now I am forced to keep on the job—finding clients, running the house and generally working myself into my grave. It is not right."

He looked so sad, this apparently respectable husband, as he sipped his drink. His wife and her sister had, after all those years of faithful service, turned out to be avaricious monsters! For him there was not the slightest realization of his having done anything wrong in his vicious, parasitic life!

Throughout the East, where so often real hunger drives girls into brothels, the unfortunate creatures who are sold or forced into prostitution are given up as lost. Except in Japan, where it is possible after a girl has served some years in a brothel, to retire and settle down into respectable life again; some even marry after their careers as prostitutes are over.

In Indo-China there was, until recently, a system under which young girls could be hired, under contract with their families, for domestic work in a neighbouring town. Sometimes they were shipped to Saigon or Hanoi (the northern capital) and, having signed an agreement to go into service for a period of several years, their "owners" placed them in brothels. The innocent victims had no chance of complaining and they soon discovered that they owed their masters for their fares both from their homes and back again. If they worked well, they could hope to earn enough to buy back their return tickets. But it took a long time.

Fees for food and lodging, for clothes and medical attention (plus interest on the initial travel expenses) were so high that few girls ever managed to buy their freedom back again. Those that did were fit for little but cleaning and other menial tasks in the houses where they had been prisoners for so long.

It was the custom in many hotels in Indo-China, before the rebellion of the local peoples and their war for independence from French rule, to have girls available for any visitor who wanted one. They were provided as part of the normal room service and were offered by the bell-boy as casually as if he were offering to bring a tray of coffee and sandwiches.

Just after the war against Japan ended, when the first American troops moved into Hanoi to take over from the Japanese, there was an example of the international uniformity of underworld practice which is worth reporting in this context.

Sergeant Rossi was an East Side boy from New York, a swarthy, tanned fellow with shoulders on him like a bull; in his army life he had a good-natured disposition and a great enthusiasm for any job that came along. He had volunteered to parachute into Hanoi with medical supplies but, as events turned out, his plane was able to land on the airfield and Rossi entered the town like a conquering hero in a commandeered truck, along with the rest of the emergency team of U.S. doctors and medical orderlies.

He and his comrades in arms worked night and day for a week or so to succour the prisoners-of-war and then, when the situation was under control, Rossi had time to look about him. It looked good to Rossi—and his whole attitude to life changed. He stopped being good-natured and adopted a tough guy manner, speaking through the side of his mouth and swaggering about, gun on hip, like a gangster. He told some of his cronies that Hanoi looked "wide open" to him and he was going to do a little "organizing" for his own good. He explained that he had been in one of the New York mobs that worked for a narcotics ring. He had also done a little "booking" (arranging appointments on commission) for a brothel circuit.

Rossi disappeared from his army mess for a few days and finally turned up at one of the town's big hotels, which was occupied by the army as a headquarters for their relief work, with a dazzling blonde on his arm.

He soon had parties of soldiers arranged for evenings in Hanoi's cabarets, where, he said, he had lined up a string of girls who were no longer employed by the Japanese officers and were anxious to make new friends with the victorious Allies. Rossi had organized his own prostitution racket. In five weeks in Hanoi he claimed to have made 60,000 piastres (then worth about £10,000) which he would take back to America as a "bank" to float a cabaret in New York.

The girls he had working for him were mainly Europeans—French, White Russian, Polish and Hungarian. They all told stories of having drifted East before the war to Shanghai, where they had been interned by the Japanese and then shipped to Hanoi. They were veterans, but they all accepted Rossi and let him take a percentage of their earnings as though he had a natural right to be their master.

Rossi, for his part, was no fool. He had told the girls that without his protection they would be either gaoled by the American authorities, or so savagely handled by the primitive Chinese troops, who were on their way to occupy the country, that their only hope of survival was to place their destinies in his hands.

Although they shared little English between them, Rossi, the booker from New York, and the prostitutes from Europe understood each other immediately. The pattern of the miniature vice racket Rossi ran in Hanoi was just a small scale model of the system as it operates everywhere else in the underworld.

None of the girls in Hanoi claimed they had been victims of "white slavers" incidentally. They had all been prostitutes in their own countries before they had begun their voyaging to the Orient. They were able to speak freely to Rossi. There was no sinister boss threatening them with violence if they did not say what he wanted them to. Had they wished, they could have claimed protection from the United States army authorities who came to take over the interim control of the city and they could have demanded repatriation to Europe. But none did this. They welcomed the arrival of Rossi and his under-world gang-boss methods which, to the women, were a happy return to a natural order of living in which they knew their place and were resigned to it.

There are some stand-over men in Arabic and African territories who still collect groups of innocent girls and shepherd them into brothels, but in Europe and America the penalties for abduction are too great for the pimps to risk breaking the law. They have no need to resort to force, particularly since the war uprooted millions of people from their homes and drove tens of thousands of women into prostitution for the sake of survival.

In Japan the problem of prostitution is entirely different from that in the western world. It has been the tradition for centuries for starving Japanese peasants, in their grim and desperate struggle to survive, to sell one or more of their daughters into brothel slavery in the so-called *greenhouses*, the official prostitution houses where the girls are trained in a rigid code of social behaviour to fit them for their task of bringing solace, both mental and physical, to their customers. This, to western eyes, shockingly callous parental behaviour among the peasants, is explained by the relentless economic pressure that crushes the poorer classes. Rather than sell his fields, a father will sacrifice a daughter and, in so doing, preserve the identity of his family which can thus remain as a land-owning unit in society.

It is evident that the Japanese view the plight of the greenhouse girls with realism and sympathy. If a geisha girl can save enough to buy her freedom, it is possible for her to later marry and raise a family without any extreme taint from her earlier record. Prostitution is an industry in Japan, to a great extent well supervised and officially controlled. During the war in the Pacific, the Japanese sent batches of greenhouse girls to their overseas troops on many scattered islands to keep up the soldiers' morale.

The huge brothel business in South America is explained, to some extent, by the social customs based on Spanish and Portuguese convention. These place strict limits on the free association of men and women before marriage. Respectable families guard their daughters closely and the availability of prostitutes has come to be regarded as a form of protection for women of virtue. Although prostitution was declared illegal in Argentina in 1936, President Peron allowed brothels to reopen in 1955. The immense increase in sex offences during the ban on semi-official prostitution forced the reversion to licensed houses.

Brothel-keepers in Argentina evolved what amounted to a trade organization or guild—the Zvi Migdal. This society was formed to restrict the trade to chains of houses within the syndicate. It forced unwanted competitors out of business, established (and policed) price lists and other conditions which were regarded as regular "trade practices". The Zvi Migdal was dominated by migrants from Europe and it made sure that any new organizers in the business came from circles in "the old countries".

The society lent money to approved borrowers (often retired prostitutes who were set up as "Madames" in new brothels) and developed particularly powerful contacts with the police forces, without whose patronage the brothel-keepers would not have made half the profits they did. When the anti-prostitution law came into force in 1936, most of the Zvi Migdal members transferred their enterprises to Brazil where the association now flourishes most happily. In Sao Paulo the prostitution racketeers have founded their own bank, they enjoy the best of liaison with the police (who are often pimps) and the society even maintains its own section of a big cemetery. The committee of management is elected with the strictest formality and the society's president wields considerable power in civic affairs.

From their monopoly of prostitution, the underworld leaders in Brazil are able to branch out into other rackets with the greatest of ease. Having paid once for police patronage, they use this influence to help themselves in many other ways. There is no richer field for underworld initiative and enterprise than in the brothels of Brazil.

In America, as in Britain, houses of prostitution are illegal, but the "call-girl" racket is just a method of running a brothel business without a brothel. It is difficult for the police to raid a telephone number, but customers can order any quantity, shape and size of women they please once they have been approved by the agents who handle this trade so smoothly and profitably.

This is the luxury section of the business, with a fifty dollar charge for "appearance money" and another fifty dollar bill if the assignment involves anything more than the provision of pleasant company and conversation.

Brothels, disguised as private homes or clubs and kept as inconspicuous as possible, exist in some States of America. Many of the earlier gang-lords who made millions from the business were frightened out of it by the Mann Anti-White Slavery Act, a piece of legislation introduced by the Federal Government to prohibit the conveyance of prostitutes across State borders. There is a new pattern developing now in the U.S. vice rackets and the extent and power of its grip is not likely to be revealed until there is another complete clean-up like the one staged by Thomas E. Dewey twenty years ago.

France's system of open houses, before the war, was an official supervision which included health checks at regular intervals and the payment of special taxes. Many French brothels were, and are, privately owned and operated as small businesses. Many of the proprietors are Corsicans, former underworld characters, whose idea of leading a quiet life in retirement from the hurly-burly of crime is to manage a string of girls in a discreet fashion, maintain good relations with the local police, and let the rest of the world go by.

Britain's system of constant police surveillance, almost regular arrest (and medical inspection) and fines for soliciting is a method that does not work at all. The great majority of British prostitutes operate as street-walkers and the dim-lit lanes and alleys within a narrow radius of the glare of Piccadilly Circus form probably the most famous prostitution area in the world. Many of these women are French or Belgian.

Their managers have devised an interesting method to prevent the girls being deported. This would be their fate automatically after arrest, if it could be established that they were not British citizens. Marriages are arranged to British subjects. This privilege is available at considerable cost, but funds are always available as long as there is a good prospect of the woman paying the money back with interest once she can operate freely and securely as a British citizen. The "husband" disappears immediately after the wedding and is, no doubt, not particularly inconvenienced by having a foreign-born wife. After all, she is not likely to make any claims on him once he has served his purpose and the man can forget this clandestine union with the greatest ease. But the girl who has raised the loan becomes more or less the property of her financial backer; she is an investment which pays off very handsomely.

One of the risks brothel customers, or street-walker's clients take is of being robbed. This thieving is a safe prospect for the prostitute and her friends for the victims are not likely to go rushing to the police to complain. The less known about their furtive purchase of love, the better; that is generally the attitude of the customer. But there are many tricks played by the prostitute who has a pickpocket accomplice, or belongs to a pimp who uses his girls as bait for cunning robbery. Some girls are expert "hooks" themselves, especially the street-walkers.

In war-time Kunming, in Western China, one group of brothel-keepers stole thousands of dollars from their American servicemen customers by means of the "false wall" gambit. The technical details of this ruse are simple enough, but the Chinese added to it an expert performance of deadpan denial which ensured that their trickery was never able to be proved against them.

In the soft, grey dawn of a Kunming spring morning, when even the jam-packed, blue-clad bustle of Chin Pi Lu, the city's main street, was not yet astir, the slightly staggering figure of a U.S. major made its way over the uneven cobbles.

Every few yards, when he reached the corner of one of the many narrow lanes that lead from the main avenue, he paused and peered anxiously at the building fronts. But their empty mud-plaster walls, with shuttered windows and barred doors, told him nothing. He was searching for the house he had been in all night and his search was a desperate one; he had discovered, as his head cleared a little in the cool blue air of the morning, that his wallet was missing. In it had been more than 1,200 American dollars (then worth 36,000 Chinese dollars) a fortune to the thief who had stolen it.

The major was humiliated as well as anxious. He had spent the night with a charming girl, in what he thought had been a respectable family apartment over a noodle and grocery shop and he was determined to find it again and demand his money back. He found it at last. Although he shouted and swore at the sleepy old woman who answered the door, he could not get her to admit that she had ever seen him before. But he recognized her and he went away vowing that he would be back with the military police to get justice. He had been able to locate the building among all the almost identical neighbouring houses, only because he had left his jeep (which he had at first forgotten) parked in front of the doorway. Now he replaced the distributor arm he had so carefully removed the night before, and drove back angrily to his quarters.

As he drove away, a sudden stir of activity began behind the sleepy wall of the house. The old woman warned the owner that the *Maigwa* (American) would be back with police. The owner knew what to do. He ordered all the women in the establishment out of the building, to lose themselves in the town until the trouble was over. Then he rapidly tore down the walls of two of the bedrooms (they were really little more than paper-thin plaster screens and easily moved section by section into the ceiling-loft) and with the aid of his coolies completely refurnished the now much larger boudoir.

The beds were changed, the drapes replaced, the original furniture taken downstairs and different chairs and tables installed. By the time the military police returned with the major, the entire upper floor was different. In the first place there was only one room now, instead of two, and in it were working three cross-legged tailors who sewed industriously all the time the policemen and the major were there.

The major had no trouble entering the house. The old woman was not the same one he had interrogated earlier that day, but she led the big Americans up the dingy staircase without making much more than a token fuss.

"It was the second room on the left," the major was saying, as he ran ahead up the stairs. "I know this is the house. I marked the door."

But there was only one bedroom now. And the proprietor appeared angrily to demand what was going on. The major said he had been robbed there the previous night and wanted to know which floor he was on.

"The first floor. There is only one," the proprietor explained through an interpreter.

"Don't give me that," yelled the major, "where's the two little bedrooms? And where's that little slopey bastard, Wong, who brought me up the drinks?"

"We have no other rooms. I know of no Wong," the proprietor said softly.

The major was rattled. "Where's that girl of yours? The one with the gold front tooth?" he demanded, but his voice lacked its former angry conviction.

"No girls here," the Chinese said. "This is a tailoring shop."

The interpreter took the major aside for a moment and whispered: "Take it easy, Major. The old guy is pretty angry and says he's going to headquarters if we don't get the hell out of here."

The major peered at the walls of the room in bewilderment. "I'll swear this is the building I was in. But maybe . . . I don't know. There were two rooms, see, just at the top of those stairs."

His voice dwindled into baffled silence. Then he turned

sharply and clattered down the stairs, signing to the police patrol to follow him. They roared away in their jeeps and did not come back again.

This trick of disguising a room and denying all knowledge of any victim who complained was an invulnerable defence against the authorities. But not many victims got even as far as the major did. Most could never recall which house they had slept in and very few were prepared to admit they had been with a prostitute when they were robbed. This trick is an international one among brothel-keepers in Asia and the Middle East, where, to European eyes, everything is strange. Add a little alcohol to befuddle the victim's wits, and the defence is fool-proof; only fools try to break it down anyway.

The European prostitution managers recruit their girls from dozens of fields—dance-halls, wine-and-dine cafes, the choruses of cheap theatres and music-halls anywhere there are attractive and somewhat simple girls in search of glamour and easy money. The pimps supply a steady stream of recruits as they bring in their victims either as a straight-out business deal, or more gradually as "friends" who like parties and, under the influence of drink and noise, can be persuaded to be submissive not only to their own escorts but to casual acquaintances with whom their escorts leave them unattended during the course of the evening.

It takes only one or two occasions like this for the relationship between the pimp and his girl to be firmly established; if she objects he may threaten to expose her indiscreet behaviour to her family, or, in some cases, he beats her into obedience. In a few weeks the shame is hidden beneath a fear, and it is not long before resignation takes the place of both fear and shame. As soon as this happens, the pimp can leave the unfortunate woman to work for him and seek about him for fresh material.

The pimps are just little cogs in the wheel of the racket; they collect only a small percentage of the illicit earnings and must pass most of it into the hands of the men and women who own the houses. When the gangs are really big, the brothel-keepers must pay tribute to "the boss" whose agents keep a careful check on the madam's turnover and are responsible for keeping the tribute up to a set standard beyond which it must never fall.

Contrary to the general principle that most prostitutes come from the lower income groups and lower social levels, the male prostitute is generally possessed of a more affluent and certainly better educated background. The main breeding ground of perversion is in the prisons, particularly in Europe, but the incredibly decadent institution of male prostitution is established firmly only in Berlin.

Before the war this particularly nasty trade flourished openly in Germany's capital where it was the fashion among many Nazi officers to support a "male friend".

These professional perverts were called *puppenjungen*, or "dolly boys", and they needed no trademark to make it clear what business they were in. They paraded up and down the famous Kurfurstendam or Unter der Linden as extravagant and tragic caricatures of humanity; they were nothing but figures of coarse fun to the crowds in which they mingled—except, of course, to the half-crazed bullies who sought them. Male prostitution is a small back-water of the trade, but its very exclusiveness makes it a rich prospect for ruthless exploiters of vice. To the high prices demanded for such special services is added the frequent opportunity for blackmailing.

Male prostitution is of importance in the underworld rackets only because it offers an area of contact for blackmailing prospects, a branch of criminal activity that requires considerable judgment, and careful planning if it is to be carried out successfully. The victims are, after all, otherwise intelligent and often influential citizens.

Prostitution, as a whole, is not only the most widespread form of vice, but is one that lends itself most easily to be organized. And it is with the organized aspects of crime that we are interested in this survey of the underworld.

7

bank-robbers and safe-breakers

OF all types of crime, robbing banks is viewed by the public with least distaste. There is something almost sporting about a bandit who, with only one or two accomplices, takes on the task of holding up several men at pistol point, takes bagfuls of money and then gets away before the police can catch him. If the coup is carried out without anyone getting hurt, nobody seems to be seriously annoyed apart from the bank governors, the insurance companies and police in whose territory the raid occurred.

Indeed in some areas of America, local residents (some of them, perhaps, in debt to the robbed bank) have been known to shelter the thieves and to aid their escape by pretending not to have seen them. Why this should be is a little mystifying, particularly as the bank-robbers are often the most ruthless of the underworld's gunmen and shoot down innocent men to make good their escape if anything goes wrong with their plans.

Bank-robbers are thieves and sometimes murderers, and any public sympathy for them as courageous and reckless young men is sadly misplaced. They take as few chances as they possibly can. They go into action knowing that they might have to kill a man to save their own skins.

Although bank-robbers are essentially lone operators, they draw heavily on the underworld's resources. They use the underworld's network of information, its huge hide-out system and its supply of car thieves, gunmen and spies more than any other type of criminal. They are the commandos of crime, and because of the big rewards they collect while they are at large, they can, and do, hire the most vicious specialists in the underworld.

America has produced the most efficient bank bandits and their efficiency is based on the power of gunmen. Before the

American underworld developed, bank robbing was a career for only the most patient and daring of safe-breakers. Better steel, improved locks and alarm systems made the game increasingly hard, but guns gave the bank-bandit a means of frontal attack in which cold-blooded shooting instead of skill won the day.

America's bank-robbers have thrown up dozens of experts in this department of crime, men like Willie ("The Actor") Sutton, Blackie Audett (forty years in the business, most of it on the run or in prison), John Dillinger, and a man who went by the name of Danny Daniels. In their hey-day they moved about America as freely as birds, with a hide-out in almost every city, with friends right across the country to lend them money, to get guns and cars and to help them stage a raid at almost any time. The bank-robbers paid, and still pay, well for this "friendship". Even when they do well for a year or so, they seldom have more than a few thousand dollars to show for all their daring and "enterprise".

Robbing a bank, in the modern manner, calls for a lot of qualities. It calls for patience, thorough and painstaking observation, detailed knowledge of bank routine, close study of the traffic conditions in and around the building to be raided.

The robber must arrange in advance a rendezvous with friends who will handle the "hot" money.

Such qualities, applied to the ordinary business of legal living, could make a good bank-robber a success in almost any calling. But there is one virtue the otherwise clever and efficient bandit lacks—respect for other people; the character to adjust himself to the rules of the game of honest living.

It is the fashion these days to explain much criminal behaviour as nothing but a problem of poor adjustment to life in the criminal's youth. These unfortunate characters, so some experts in psychology claim, would have presented no problem to society at all had they only been given a fair chance in their childhood. They have a yearning for excitement that everyday work does not supply; they are just misguided and not really evil at all. But these theories are of little comfort to the widow of a bank clerk who has had his life ended with a bullet for doing nothing more than his job.

Banks, particularly the smaller branches in country towns, are fairly easy to rob. A few weeks before the day on which they strike, the bank-robber and his accomplices move into the town and settle into a local hide-out. In larger cities, of course, they stage their raids and do their planning from the underworld's traditional headquarters, the melinas.

First the bandits must discover which day and which hour is the best to strike. Perhaps it is the day on which the bank has larger funds of ready cash than usual to meet some local pay-roll demand. They check on the police strength and the roster for duty; in some cases a local contact gives them all this information.

If they have to get it themselves, one of them must move about in the unsuspecting community while the others remain in hiding. The "front" usually adopted by the scout is generally that he is a travelling salesman, or a real estate speculator sizing up a new area for the investment of his money. They do not show any particular imagination in the roles they choose, but this is all to the good, as small town people are more likely to accept such run-of-the-mill characters without much suspicion. Anything more exotic would attract far too much interest.

Willie Sutton, whose method was one of classic simplicity, used to arrive early at the bank, just after the first employee let himself in. Then Sutton would hold this first arrival at gun-point and bail up the rest of the staff, sometimes half a dozen men, as they came in the door. When he had forced one of them to hand over the keys of the strong room, he would shepherd them all into a small room and lock them in while he collected a suitcase full of notes. He worked with fantastic speed and great coolness, his schedule calculated to the very minute. Once he had the money he would leave in great haste, leap into a waiting car and get away with several minutes start on the police. Sutton was a great artist and never worked with more than one or two helpers; he was known as Willie "The Actor" for his clever impersonations in "casing his jobs."

Others work as teams, with two or three gunmen holding up the bank staff and any customers who might be in the building. Other confederates are outside in the escape car and watching to raise the alarm should the police happen to get wind of the raid. Sometimes they take a bank employee with them as a hostage when they leave; if they are not chased within a certain time, the hostage will be dumped unharmed. If the police fire too soon the hostage will be dumped as a corpse. There are not many bank managers who are prepared to lose the life of one of their staff for the sake of a few thousand dollars which the insurance companies will have to make up anyway.

But frequently, one of the bandit team is "a wild operator", a man whose itchy trigger finger is unpredictable—especially if some member of the bank staff should resent being held up and show signs of fight. It is then the "good clean fun" of bank robbing suddenly switches to the ugly crime of murder.

As in war, audacity is an essential for the success of a bank raid. Most people tend to gape unbelievingly when they are held up at gun-point, all thought of resistance dulled in their minds. Because the robbers can never hope to have more than a few minutes grace before the alarm is raised, the average man never dreams anyone will have the cheek to stage a robbery. But a few minutes is all the bandits ever expect in their gamble against the law and, given the chance to start running only a mile or so ahead of the police, they are prepared to go to work.

Many of the more skilful bank-robbers plan their raids, rehearse their teams of thugs and adopt all the resources of theatrical make-up and timing to help them succeed. But no one can predict how a man will behave in a crisis, and no bandit can forsee the unexpected dislocation of normal routine in a bank. The early or late arrival of just one member of the staff, the unorthodox call of any of the bank's customers, can undo weeks of foresight and anticipation.

In one instance, the bank-robbers worked out every detail, right down to making a detailed plan of the wiring of the alarm system. It took them weeks of patient reconnaissance to tabulate every procedure in the office, and they even knew which of the bank's staff would be on leave on the day they struck. Their plan worked like clockwork.

They entered the bank one minute after it opened. One bandit went to the right inside the door and cut the alarm system wires that were connected to the police station; another went to the left to hold up the clerical staff and a third moved swiftly into the manager's office to disconnect the telephone,

The ring-leader scooped 50,000 dollars into a suitcase from the ledge behind the teller's counter, where he had been told it would be resting. The team backed out the front door, leaving the staff locked in the strong room. It took them exactly three minutes, as planned.

But the police were waiting for them on the doorstep and in the gun battle that followed all but one of the bandits were arrested. The one who was not arrested was killed.

They did not discover until their trial what went wrong. It was a little thing—but enough to wreck the entire project. At the time they struck, the alarm system of the bank should have been given its weekly test ring to the police station. The bandits, had they known this, could have let any one of the staff ring the alarm—or rung it themselves—and they would have had no interference whatsoever. But the alarm bells did not ring and the police had only to look down the street to see a car parked outside the front door, a car they had never seen before. Within moments they were alerted and on the job.

The headlines are always big and black and bold when a bank is robbed, but the bandits are often caught within a few days without any fuss and the public never finds out just how it was done. The police have friends in the underworld, just as criminals do. Also there are often quite a selection of charges to be preferred against the bank-robbers and their crews—charges like driving without correct licences, being in possession of stolen cars (the normal method of travel for bank raiders), or the infringement of some local bye-law, such as speeding along a main street, or even parking in a prohibited area.

The women these criminals attract are a constant problem, as they are only happy when they are being given expensive presents. Even these do not bind them to any lasting loyalty if things become difficult. The great army of extortion experts, the petty parasites and the rivalries of other gangsters make the bank-robber with a big haul an easy mark for dozens of his underworld fellows. There are also the police.

No matter how clever the planning or how intricate the ruses used to confuse the victims, nearly all bank-robbers spend more time in prison than out of it. Many people argue that the high-powered American system has taken all the artistry out of bank robbing. The old craft of safe-breaking, it is suggested, is dead.

It is true that the old craft of safe-breaking has fewer experts than it once had, but it still provides a good living for any underworld character who understands locks, combinations and the use of gelignite or acetylene torches, to penetrate a steel door. The early safe-breakers were, in fact, illegal locksmiths and this trade even to-day is not taught at technical schools on the ground that such instruction would soon make it a school for burglars. The craft is normally handed on from father to son, or master to apprentice, in the old tradition of workmanship.

But there are still locksmiths in the underworld. Their assignments are sometimes limited to opening doors and padlocked gateways these days, but the best of them can still, and often do, open safes.

Modern safes are a vastly improved version of the safes of fifty years ago. But there are still many old safes in use, and wherever there are safes there are valuables and money.

This does not mean that modern safes cannot be rifled. They can, but the old method of opening them on the spot has been largely discarded in favour of removing the entire safe and breaking it open at the thief's leisure with explosives or metal-cutting tools and torches.

To remove a safe, a gang must first get access to it, and it is here that the lock-picker is valuable. He can open any door, unless it is specially wired or built of solid steel. The lock-picker enters the building, the thieves remove the safe to waiting trucks and drive it away.

In the early safe-breaking days a good man could operate almost alone and rely entirely on the skill in his fingers and his head to break the safe open wherever it stood. The locksmith, with his bag of strange, delicate wire probes and skeleton keys, generally can tickle the most intricate lock mechanism open in a few moments.

Modern safe-makers developed stronger doors, and better locks. These operated by means of a combination of lever movements which could be solved only by knowing the exact number of turns to give a spinning dial. The safe-breakers, in their turn, developed a band of specialists who, with sand-papered finger tips to increase their sensitivity of touch, could twist dials so swiftly and deftly (listening meanwhile to the tiny, muffled thuds inside the lock as levers fell into place) that they could solve pretty well any combination. It took time and patience and cool nerves.

Then came the design of even stronger safes, with even more intricate combinations. Some now have locks which, if disturbed by an explosion or a locksmith's probe, automatically shoot other bolts inside the safe door and lock it more securely than ever. The safe-breakers, however, have learned new skills with electric drills. They can bore a lock from its bearings by grinding out the screws which hold the mechanism in place.

The safe-breakers' present problem is to evolve methods of moving safes quickly and silently from the buildings in which they are housed. To do this they make use of all the modern equipment for lifting—mechanical hoists, powered trolleys and heavy duty vehicles. This sort of gear needs expert handling if the booty is to be moved rapidly and with a minimum of fuss. Safe-breaking gangs are now larger, because of this.

The operations are planned with immense care to ensure that the removal team have time to function before an alarm is given.

When the first safe-combinations became too difficult to solve within half an hour or so, the safe-breakers became expert dynamiters. This is a skilled trade in itself. A good dynamiter can remove the door or the lock of a safe as neatly as a man opening a can of sardines and do the job without doing any damage to surrounding walls or floors. Controlled blasts of this nature are routine jobs for experts.

But even the most skilled blasting became out-dated when the magic flame of oxy-acetylene torches enabled men to cut through metal quickly. Here again the underworld kept pace with modern technology and the torch men took over from the explosives expert.

The story of safe-breaking is a continuous record of improving skills, but modern "burglar proof" safes are costly and far too expensive for all but the larger firms. There are tens of thousands of old safes still in use, and the old skills are still much in demand.

Perhaps the most famous of pre-war safe-breakers in Europe was the Pole, Czichocki, whose ability to gain access to safes and then break them open was legendary. He had studied engineering as a young man and was an expert tunneller as well as a brilliant safe-breaker.

Czichocki, like other "tank men" (as safe breakers are known in some quarters) was often called to other countries on special jobs, but it was while he was working on a project in his own country—the robbing of the Bank of Poland at Czestochowa—that he was finally caught.

It was an ambitious project. He had to tunnel beneath a roadway from the basement of a shop opposite the bank, and push the tunnel through to a point exactly under the floor of the strong-room to get at the safe.

The tunnel progressed rapidly, with Czichocki digging out soil each night and having it carted away in baskets each morning once his own basement could hold no more. All went well until one day one of the accomplices was recognized as a "wanted" man by detectives and the whole project was revealed.

The tunnel, it was found, was perfectly constructed and lit by electricity. It had taken the lean and bearded Pole and three helpers six months to dig it. It was a remarkable achievement. All it earned him was five years in gaol.

The underworld fraternity of safe-breakers is a tightly interlocked group of specialists. A good safe-breaker, whether an expert in explosives, oxy-acetylene work or straight, old-fashioned lock picking, is often called from one country to another, just as Czichocki was in his prime. But many prefer to work alone or, when they really need assistance, to hire accomplices merely to keep watch and generally help in the business of escape and disposal of the booty.

A Belgian safe-breaker, known as Simon the Painter, pulled off many successful safe-breaking robberies in Brazil working alone. He sometimes used a very old and simple trick to help him enter premises.

Simon the Painter got his nickname (safe-breakers rarely go by their real names) because of the way he used his old trade to provide him with a harmless and respectable front while he planned his raids. He was a sign-writer and he found this a most useful attribute when spying out the lie of the land.

Simon specialized in robbing jeweller's safes, particularly when the shop was on the ground floor of a building that had other rooms to rent upstairs. In fact Simon would seldom touch a job unless the construction and the design of the building fitted in with his method of entering the victim's premises from above.

His safe-breaking method became almost a ritual with the passing of the years. Simon never liked to make a mess on the job. He disapproved of explosives and metal-cutting torches as crude, unimaginative techniques for opening a safe.

He was an artist. He could pick a lock as swiftly as any man alive and he liked to work neatly, leaving no trace of his theft—except an empty shelf inside a safe and a small pile of debris from the broken ceiling. The debris was always stacked in a corner before he departed through the front door into the street.

Simon could have picked most of the door-locks on the premises he entered, but he was a little nervous about working at the front of a shop and he would wait weeks, if necessary, to cut his way into the store from above or from an adjacent room. Sometimes Simon managed to rent the room directly above his target—an ideal arrangement because it meant he could work at his leisure.

The essential item in all Simon's preparations for a safe robbery was a large umbrella. Having bored a small hole through the jeweller's ceiling from the room above, Simon would thrust his umbrella through it and then open it, thus making a most useful "apron" to catch the rest of the brick and plaster and wood splinters which fell away as the hole was made big enough for Simon to get through. When the hole was big enough, and the open umbrella full of debris, Simon would lower the laden umbrella to the floor in the shop below on a string and drop in after it, falling as silently as a cat to the floor below. The umbrella kept the whole job tidy, the way Simon liked it, and it also kept the debris from falling noisily into the darkened shop below.

Once inside the shop Simon would pick the safe-lock, extract the valuables and depart as silently as he had come.

He moved about South America very freely for some years and lived very well on the proceeds of about one robbery a year, but his devotion to the old European methods at last caused his donwfall.

The umbrella trick was new to Brazil and the Argentine but a German policeman who came to settle in Sao Paulo realized what was happening as soon as he saw the first neat pile of debris after a Simon robbery and he remembered the method of Simon the Painter.

He learnt that a signwriter had moved into a certain building in the main shopping area of the city. He watched the signwriter at work, then he noticed that there was a jeweller's shop on the ground floor.

The policeman spent many nights locked inside the shop until at last he saw what he had been waiting for—a black umbrella probing through a small hole in the ceiling. The umbrella opened out, Simon dropped to the floor and the policeman pounced.

Simon the Painter was gaoled for three years, but had the German waited a little longer and allowed Simon to open the safe and take the diamonds he was after, the sentence would have been much more severe. Simon was able to plead that he had stolen nothing and that his offence was merely illegal entry. It was not much consolation, but it was something.

Simon was a lone hand but other safe-breakers who use the tunnelling technique on a larger scale have brought off some big hauls. Perhaps the biggest and most ambitious project was the "Asphalt Case" in Germany when a gang succeeded in breaking into a bank in Cologne. They employed a particularly brazen ruse.

They dug a hole in the footpath outside the bank in broad daylight and erected over it one of those steel frames, covered with canvas, which are normally used by telephone mechanics working on underground cables. With this flimsy cover over their initial hole, the tunnellers proceeded to dig their way under the bank's wall, throwing up the soil to be loaded on to a waiting lorry. All went well, amid the casually interested glances of passers-by, and at nightfall the gang completed its tunnel and entered the bank. The bank did not reveal what was stolen (thinking, perhaps, that to disclose their loss might start a run on their funds) but it was understood the gang made an immense haul from their daring hole in the asphalt.

Gangs, like the one which carried out the "Asphalt Case" robbery, plan their jobs for weeks before they go into action.

Like the armed bandits in America, they study every angle of the problem from inside and outside the building. They draw detailed plans of the premises, they study the wiring of any alarm systems, and they discover what funds the safe will contain.

The large gangs have their own team of electricians who do nothing but devise ways of defeating automatic alarms. One group in Berlin, which had an importing office as a "front" headquarters, used to ask the burglar alarm makers to install the latest system for them—and then study how it could be defeated. In this way the underworld's technical knowledge kept abreast with the latest developments in crime prevention among the alarm manufacturers.

The knowledge gleaned by every cracksman is passed on and shared, eventually, with every other safe-breaker. This habit of doing each other favours is traditional in the underworld. It pays big dividends when things get tough. It might be years since one criminal helped another but the debt is never forgotten. When the time comes for the debt to be repaid the party in need of aid is seldom let down.

The system works well in America where criminals move rapidly from State to State and there is no barrier of language or nationality, as in Europe. Guns, money, cars and expert safe-breakers are a widely spread stock-in-trade throughout bank-robbing circles in the United States. Any crook who has been "out of work" (i.e. in prison) for a few years has little difficulty in getting back into action when he is released. Indeed, there is generally a job waiting for him wherever he has contacts in the great, restless, greedy community to which he belongs.

It is little wonder that the experienced criminal seldom talks to the police. His whole life depends on his loyalty to the underworld. Once a man is suspected as an informer, he is suddenly isolated and defeated—the honest world wants to have nothing to do with him and the underworld becomes full of danger and cold indifference.

There are, however, fewer informers in the safe-breaking and bank-robbing groups than in others. These men are all highly skilled, one way or another, and they do not mix at all freely with other criminals. They have too much at stake to let anyone in on a job unless he is needed for his expert knowledge. Like the banking business, the bank-robbing business could not operate without a large degree of mutual trust and credit.

Mistakes, however, do occur frequently. Perhaps one of the most ironical concerns the German partnership between two men, in Essen before the war, who had been working together for years. Their system was for one man to let the other into a building about midnight (they were both expert lock-pickers) and then return just before dawn to let the man inside out again. In this way the door of the premises remained safely locked and any police patrol would not suspect anything.

On the night the partnership foundered, the building the men were robbing was one of a group of shops in the central section of the city. The police inspected the door every half hour. There was no hitch about getting into the shop but the man whose turn it was to work inside had been a little careless about leaving his own front door open back in the flat building where he lived.

This might not have mattered particularly had the safe-breaker not been the proud owner of a dachshund, a dog of which he was deeply fond.

The dachshund, equally devoted to his master, was delighted to discover that he could, for once, get out and follow in his master's footsteps. They led, of course, to the doorway of the shop and there the dog stayed, whining and barking furiously, and scratching at the door.

The first time round the policeman merely tried to draw the dog away. But the second time the dog was still there and still frantically trying to attract attention. This time he succeeded, but it was the wrong sort of attention for the man inside. The policeman contacted the owner of the shop who came into the city immediately to see why a dog should want to enter his store at 1 o'clock in the morning.

The man inside was arrested as he worked at the safe. The wagging tail and adoring eyes of his dog were little comfort to him that night; the only consolation he had was that his partner got away safely. Seeing that they had caught a lock-smith safe-breaker, the police did not think for a moment that he might have an accomplice. They assumed he had picked the door-lock himself.

In their pride of making an arrest, they overlooked the fact that not even the cleverest lock expert can shut a door behind him and lock a padlock on the outside bolt!

No survey of safe-breaking would be complete, from the underworld point of view, without a mention of Nosko, who carried out a fabulous robbery on a Brazilian customs house after nine months' careful preparation.

Nosko got himself into the Customs office strong-room (where he knew there was a safe containing £120,000 worth of Brazilian currency) and out again without being detected. He lay low for a week or so and then, with his stolen money packed into the false bottom of a suitcase he was waiting at the Rio airport to fly to America when all his plans came unstuck. His mistress rushed into the air terminal lounge flung herself into his arms and, before he realized what was happening, tore up his passport.

She loved him too much, she said, to let him go. Her infatuation was so great that she told the police about his suitcase and Nosko was detained for some years before he could fly away. His mistress consoled herself with another lover—and the reward the police had offered for the recovery of the stolen money. Doggy and womanly devotion, it seems, do not mix well with the skilled and secret occupation of cracking safes!

The main characteristic of safe-breakers' behaviour, within the setting of the underworld community, is that, although they are in the biggest and most rewarding of the criminal "trades" they have nothing of the pose and "front" of the other main class of big money earners, the confidence men. Safe-breakers spend no time or trouble trying to build themselves a respectable reputation the way "con" men do. To the confidence man, of course, such a background is essential. It is his main asset. But the safe-breakers live and work as "people of the night". Their efficiency depends on secrecy, careful planning and the reliability of their "inside information.'

This close relationship has bred envy among some other branches of the criminal world, mainly the unskilled and violent groups. But among the safe-breakers and bank-robbers themselves their dependence on each other has produced a sense of co-operative responsibility and an unofficial, yet effective, method of supporting the families of imprisoned members by payments from a general fund. As long as the man in trouble is in good standing with the group, he can rest assured that his family will be looked after until he is released and able to work again. This and other forms of assistance among criminals is known in the underworld under the disarming title of the Old Pals Act.

In the event of arguments over the division of booty, or charges of dishonesty, the group settles its own troubles by a rough form of arbitration, and even rougher justice, in much the same way as the pickpockets with the *Courts of Honour* do. Many a wounded criminal, picked up by the police, has died refusing to reveal his attackers. This is not always loyalty to his underground breed, but an acceptance of the punishment handed out to him.

A lifetime in the criminal world removes its members so completely from the standards and ideals of normal living that it is quite beyond their powers, even when mortally wounded, to take the side of the everyday world against their comrades—and enemies—in the underworld. The much-vaunted "tough silence" of criminals, their almost universal refusal to help the police in any way, is not a form of defiant courage, but merely the result of years of conditioning. They fight society to the end as instinctively as some citizens risk death without a second thought to protect their own or their employer's property.

The so-called courage of criminals is a perverted courage. It is not a thing to be glamourised. It is a tragedy. The very same qualities that make a man an underground hero could just as easily have made him an out-standing character in normal life. All that is needed, in many cases, is a re-direction of their energies and a reformation of their standards.

This transformation has less chance of happening in prison than anywhere else. Prisons confirm the criminal in his ways, they put him more on the side of the law-breakers than the law. It is in prison that a great proportion of crime is planned. Boredom, close association between veteran and apprentice criminals and a feeling of the need for banding together in the face of adversity breeds and strengthens criminal activity.

This point has been made before, but it is particularly true in the case of safe-breakers and the other expert members of bank robbing circles. These men plot their jobs for weeks, sometimes months, and they pick their partners with infinite care. A successful operation allows them to retreat into the many backwaters and by-ways of the criminal world for a year or so before they need to go into action again. A term of prison is in many ways an ideal opportunity for some men to make new alliances and plot new triumphs.

One of the highly profitable variations of safe-breaking and bank robbing is the insurance racket. This, in many instances, is the same as an inside information job. The only difference from the outside public's point of view is that two parties to the theft are sometimes punished instead of one. The insurance racket involves a conspiracy between the owner of the safe and the crooks. The inside information robbery involves only the crooks and their "leak" within the organization that is robbed.

Insurance racket gangs provide a truly professional service when they are called in, as they often are, to get a wealthy man out of difficulties. In one case a European diamond merchant saved himself from ruin. For some time heavy gambling losses and a series of unfortunate love affairs had drained his resources, until he was forced to sell most of his stock for ready cash.

He conducted these sales without revealing them in his books, but a day of reckoning had to come. Although heavily in debt the diamond merchant never failed to keep up his big insurance policy and it was now that he turned to this investment.

A receiver well known to the diamond merchant said he could contact a gang of safe-breakers who were guaranteed to be discreet. They could, for a fee of £1,000, stage a perfectly convincing robbery. All the merchant had to do was pay them the fee in advance and then make a claim on his insurance company.

The gang was hired and carried out its raid with complete efficiency. The merchant made his claim and collected the £60,000 cover he had always kept on his stock. It was enough to clear his debts, and to leave him enough to start business again. This is just one variation of the method used in the insurance racket—the safest form of crime for the professional crooks who are called in and the safest swindle a business-man can carry out.

Another instance of cunning on a routine job illustrates how the underworld would be lost without its safe-breakers of the old lock-picking school.

This incident occurred in Paris when a gang of burglars who specialized in stripping flats were stuck for a lock expert. Their regular expert was "inside", but before they had time to replace him they learned of a particularly promising job.

A wealthy financier had left his city apartment vacant over the summer holidays, but was expected back in a day or so. The gang had to break in at short notice, or not at all.

When they got into the flat, they found a secret wall safe behind a picture and, despite their most determined efforts, were unable to break it open. They left the flat in a hurry and went to one of the underworld meeting places, a cafe, where they picked up a professional safe-breaker and rushed him back to the job.

He got to work on the wall safe, and, in a few minutes, the gang had the "take" they had planned on getting without expert aid. Experts called in suddenly on jobs like this are generally paid an agreed cut of the haul.

Earlier in this chapter, safe-breakers and bank-robbers were referred to as "the commandos of crime", as cool customers who are interested in high stakes only and yet capable of patient and thorough preparation of their many enterprises. This apparent contradiction, or combination of action and caution, seldom is found in any one criminal. But it is found in almost every partnership or gang.

The confidence men may be the artists of the underworld, but the bank-robbers and their many specialist colleagues are the aristocracy of the lawless international community. Cunning, courage and greed are the underworld's most respected qualities.

8

cardsharps and gamblers

THE underworld's interest in gambling is universal, infinitely varied and always profitable. Some of it is organized, as in the mob control of America's vast gambling rackets, and some of it entirely individual. In the case of the individual performers, their prey, for once, is hunted down as much within the underworld itself as outside among the normal public.

Criminals flourish wherever there is greed for money. Gambling, whether it is betting on numbers, cards, dice or horses, provides an element which the crook breathes as naturally as he does the air. Gambling is money for nothing and, to the underworld, money for nothing is one of the natural rights of man.

The wonderful thing about gambling, from the crook's point of view, is that the victims are robbed, cheated and exploited at their own risk. Gambling losses may not be recovered by law and crooked gambling, which is just as much theft as robbing a safe, gives the victim no legal redress at all. The only protection society offers the innocent against gambling is the prohibition of gaming dens in countries like Britain and the British Commonwealth and America. It is a prohibition which has little effect, of course, as these countries have all the gaming dens they need. In France, Belgium, Switzerland, Italy and South American countries, to name only some of the nations where a man may risk his money on the chance turn of a card or the roll of a dice, gambling is legal. In these countries customers at any cafe may call for a pack of cards and try their luck with anyone they choose.

Horse-racing, in the eyes of the law, is not a game of chance, but a sport in which good judgment and good form are supposed to make the selection of winners a matter of skill. Officially recognized and socially approved by the majority, "the Sport of Kings" provides one of the underworld's richest fields.

Every race-track has its crooks. They operate on the fringes of the sport and are always available for hire to unscrupulous owners, trainers and punters. Only by constant supervision, strict regulation and severe penalties do the reputable racing organizations of the world manage to keep racing, more or less, free from criminal influence.

It is a ceaseless struggle which gives no complete victory to the honest racing men. For every case of horse-doping, electric batteries in saddles and whips, pulled horses and dishonest practice that is uncovered by racecourse officials, there may be one or more races won by the same means.

Professional gamblers do not risk their resources, or waste their time, at race-tracks unless they are in the business. The average punter, so the gamblers claim, has more chance of winning money at roulette, baccarat or dice in a well-run casino than he ever has at a racecourse.

The casinos of Europe are glamorous places, set in luxury and designed to distract the wealthy. From Ostend to Naples, all through the glittering money belt of the Continental seaboard pleasure spots, wealthy syndicates become wealthier every day as the gambling public flock to try their luck. Among them are the professionals, the men and women who pay their living expenses by betting within strict limits and with a full knowledge of the odds. They risk nothing unless they consider they have, at least, an even chance. They risk, perhaps £10 a day. If they win on their first plunge, they stop betting. If they lose their money, they stop betting; they seldom try to recoup their losses. This gives them enough to live, to pay for their hotel rooms and their meals.

But the real profits come from the "suckers", the country people, the man or woman crazed with gambling, or the crook with easy money to wager. There is one thing common to all these types, they have a greed that blunts their shrewdness and makes them vulnerable to the expert.

The main games played at the casinos are baccarat, chemin-de-fer, roulette, trente et quarante. In South America the popular card game is *Campista*, a game somewhat like Faro, and played with three decks of cards.

The practice in European casinos is to have one Zero on the roulette wheel. This gives the house a three per cent chance of winning all bets at each turn of the wheel no matter how the luck runs on *rouge et noire* (red and black) and *pair et impair* (even numbers and odd) and individual numbers. In South America the casinos have two Zeros on their wheels; this gives the management a six per cent chance in every spin, apart from their chances of winning the other ways.

In Europe financiers control most of the casinos; in America (where such establishments are illegal, except at Las Vegas, with its famous "strip" of luxury resorts equipped with gambling rooms) the dens are run by the gangs. In South America, big business concerns and the Government share in the immense proceeds of games of chance.

It is not often that a casino loses heavily and when it does the directors suspect they have been robbed. The occasions when some honest client has a phenomenal run of luck are so infrequent that they can be written off as a business risk. The precautions against cheating taken by casino managements are elaborate, but not always fool-proof.

Among their clients there is always a proportion of crooks waiting and watching for a chance to make a dishonest killing. The victims are generally other customers, but casino managements cannot afford to have it known that they have crooks among their clients. The battle of wits against fair play never ends.

Like banks and insurance companies, casinos have few sympathizers among the public when they are robbed. One criminal coup that succeeded in Uruguay brought particular delight to the South American underworld and mild amusement to the citizens of two countries.

It happened that one management ran two casinos, one in Uruguay and the other in Brazil. At both they used identical chips for their roulette and card games, but in Brazil the chips cost the equivalent of ten cents each, in Uruguay the chips sold for one dollar. When Jacob the Lion, a widely known gambling man, learned about this he rapidly made his arrangements and put his plan into action. It was wonderfully simple, and by Jacob's standards, a perfectly legitimate deal.

He visited the Brazilian casino and bought 5,000 dollars

worth of ten cent chips; then he chartered a plane to fly him to the firm's other casino in Uruguay and cashed them. His net profit for the deal was about 40,000 dollars—and nobody could complain. But he was not able to work it again. The casino noticed the shortage of 50,000 ten cent chips in the Brazilian branch and the surplus of 5,000 dollar chips in the Uruguay establishment almost immediately. They changed their stock of chips at one of the casinos within twenty-four hours.

The setting in big casinos is admirably suited to the professional crooks who make gambling and cardsharping their business. The lavish atmosphere of places like the extravagant *Mare la Plata*, a few miles outside Buenos Aires and the *Copacabana Palace* at Rio, has a softening influence on the hardest of business brains. The circles of play, the glitter of beautiful women and sense of excitement that accompanies the making or losing of a fortune by chance suits the cool calculation of the cheat ideally.

There are many ways he can set out to make money. He can play to cheat the casino, he can select a victim from the thousands of innocent clients displayed in the gambling rooms, or he can watch a crook playing with stolen money and extort a percentage of it in exchange for silence.

In America, where the illegal gambling dens survive under police protection, the professionals operate with particular success. Here, in these lush establishments, they can be sure that many of the players are themselves crooks. Such men are living on borrowed time with stolen money. They throw their cash about recklessly.

They are never sure how long they will be at liberty to do so, and by the very nature of their own lives, they must take chances. They live by luck, the way law-abiding citizens live by caution and earnest endeavour. There is no easier "take" for a gambling crook than another criminal who happens to be in the money.

The gambling crook always operates in the comforting knowledge that, even if he is caught out, he will generally suffer no penalty apart from being thrown off the premises. To the normal man such humiliation and violence is an enormous risk, a disaster not to be contemplated, but to professional gambling crooks, it is merely a danger that goes with the job—no more alarming than the probability of ulcers for an advertising executive, or broken bones for a footballer.

The professional gambler accepts fortune and misfortune as calmly as the rest of us accept the process of growing old. If he wins, it is nothing more than he expects as the result of a well-planned operation; if he loses, he shrugs and forgets his bad luck. What is done, is done, and bemoaning ill-luck is useless. Gamblers learn to live with risks just as the ordinary city worker learns to live with heavy traffic. The gambler does not lie awake at night worrying about his luck to-morrow, any more than the city worker lies awake calculating his chances of being run over the next day.

This acceptance of loss, even of the chance of injury, breeds a calmness and a confidence without which a crooked gambler could not survive. A cardsharp must never fumble, a swindler must never hestate when the stakes are running high. Indeed it is when the victims are tense and the turn of a card means thousands that the professional is at his coolest.

This self-control, this hardened ability to think and act calmly at moments of crisis forms the whole basis of a gambling crook's existence.

The dishonest gambler's stock-in-trade includes marked cards, sleight-of-hand and shrewd judgment. That is all, but it is enough.

One of the most successful underworld gamblers in recent years was an elderly Swiss, a tall, slightly bent man with arthritic hands and a disease of the eyes which obliged him to wear dark glasses.

He has retired from the Continent now to live out his last years in Sao Paulo, well-off and content to do nothing but dabble in a few illegal currency deals. But when he travelled the casinos of Europe, he was a pathetic figure, lonely and always a mere onlooker at the play which seemed to fascinate him. His failing eyesight, he said, when some sympathetic person engaged him in conversation, prevented his taking a part in the fun. But the tension and the excitement of the baccarat tables were a stimulation he could not bear to leave.

This man made a fortune by "merely watching" baccarat. He worked with an accomplice. Baccarat, as played in European casinos, is a game in which twelve or fourteen punters sit around a table. The house holds the bank and a croupier deals the cards. Spectators may bet as the game proceeds, staking their money on any card a player receives.

The elderly Swiss with the unfortunate affliction of the eyes would watch the play for several nights before he put his method into action. By the time he was ready to operate, he would have "switched" a pack of the croupier's cards, substituting a marked pack for the normal ones.

This he sometimes did by pure sleight-of-hand, sometimes by arrangement. But in the marked pack the cards were distinguished by large signs in special coloured ink, visible only through dark red glasses. To the person of normal sight there was no sign to be seen, even under the closest inspection, of the coloured marks.

The Swiss stood near the croupier, placed his accomplice among the spectators on the far side of the table. When the vital cards were dealt, face down to a player, he would signal the accomplice. Immediately the accomplice would place his bet and collect. It was a remarkable bit of team work.

Their bets on the newly-dealt cards had to appear spontaneous, the signal had to be disguised a dozen different ways and never be repeated twice running. The accomplice had to place a few losing bets among the winning ones to allay all suspicion.

One night of winning by this method, and the Swiss and his partner would move on to another resort, wait their chance for another evening of collusion and clean up again. When the Swiss left Europe to settle in South America, his eyesight seemed to improve. These days he no longer wears dark spectacles. The red-tinted pair he wore on the nights when he was "working" are his most treasured souvenirs.

Many people have heard his story and refused to believe it. They cannot conceive how such a ruse could possibly be arranged and carried out successfully not once but many times. It is this element of "impossibility" which aids such crooks in their methods. If they try something no one imagines they could carry out, their battle is won. No one is on guard for the apparently impossible.

Sometimes the gamblers sit in on a game and palm cards

dealt to them, replacing the cards they receive with others. To do this they must have identical packs of cards and they must know exactly when to act.

These men can make cards disappear and appear in their hands with all the skill of the best magicians and illusionists, and do it within closer range of their audience than the magician is ever called upon to do. It is their timing, the sense of tension among other members in the game, which so often rewards them with success.

Such tricksters never operate when the game is well run and all the players have their wits about them. They wait until late in the night when attention lags a little and the consuming fever of the gaming table dulls the normally acute perceptions of the players. Their frauds are discovered only when the casino finds it has extra cards in some of the packs. Some casinos have adopted the practice of using larger cards than the usual size to protect themselves and their legitimate clients. The cards are too big to be palmed.

But casinos and gambling dens would provide crooks with a living even if they did not play in the set games. Such places are ready-made assembly points for the people the crooks are waiting for—the amateurs, the men and women who let themselves get slightly fuddled by drink, and, surprisingly, the hard-headed gambling experts who so fancy their ability to look after themselves that they become over-confident.

The "chivalry" of gambling is, in itself, a powerful aid to the criminal gambler. A man who is playing for high stakes knows it is not done to back away from a challenge; it is considered a loss of face to refuse a wager in many circles—particularly where play is fast and stakes are high. Get a "sucker" in such a setting, flatter him a little and let him win considerable sums of money; then he is ready for picking by the professionals.

These men, of course, do not gamble at all. There is no element of chance in their work. They operate as business men. They invest their money only when they are sure of making a profit and they are prepared to wait with infinite patience for the moment to strike. Their position in the underworld is unusual. They are not entirely on the side of the lawless against the law; many of their victims are criminals who happen to be in the money. Gamblers regard any game as fair game, and do not have the same sense of unity with other crooks as most classes in the underworld do. They are not at all dependent on the underworld's key men—receivers, gunmen and forgers—the way most other criminals are. They do not experience the same risk of imprisonment and legal punishment, but are merely parasites living off other parasites.

Their main contacts with the underworld in general are limited to discovering where the money lies in any given group. On the other hand, they know that the underworld cannot live without gambling and that one of the essential traits in a member of criminal society is his readiness to take a chance. A crook's life is founded on taking risks.

This relationship between the gamblers and the criminals, like all human relationships, is a two-way situation. The inevitable inter-dependence makes the gambler a little more tolerant of his criminal victims, a little less ruthless than he is with "squares"—the law-abiding citizens whose stupidity in working for their money makes them worthy only of exploitation. Many criminal dens send out for a cardsharper if a "mug" player appears and the whole group stands by while the professional goes to work.

Cardsharps employ four techniques—marked cards, stripped cards, codes and sleight-of-hand. The marking of cards is a profession in itself, if the skill in being able to read the markings is included as part of this special division of robbery.

The cardsharp's basic skill, whatever system he favours, is the art of prestidigitation—juggling of cards. This skill, polished to a fantastic degree of perfection by many crooks, is acquired only after years of constant practice and single-minded devotion to the task. There is little point in marking cards, from the cardsharp's point of view, if he cannot also manipulate them to make them fall as he wishes.

The method of marking cards follows almost as many patterns as there are crooks in the business. The tiniest of scratches, no larger than pin-points, are all the expert needs (or dares) to have as his guide. These minute signs, arranged among the close-printed pattern of the normal card, need indicate only a few key cards in the pack to give the crook an immense advantage.

The only way the novice can detect the marks is to bend the

back of the card at an angle against a strong light. Then, and only then, can the tiny indentations or raised particles of the card's reverse surface be detected. But cardsharps, who spend as much time handling, doctoring and looking at cards as the best concert pianists spend at practice each day, can tell by a rapid glance or a delicate feeling of the card just what its "message" is. But without marked cards or anything else in their favour, they are surprisingly poor card players.

There are few conventions about marking cards, but it is safe to say that court cards—the Ace, King, Queen and Jack—are indicated, as a rule, by marks along the top and bottom edge of the cards. The values of the other cards—from tens down to wos—are revealed by marks down the side of the cards.

Having got into a game with a deck of marked cards, the victim's only hope of cutting his losses is to stop playing. But the art of cardsharping is not to let the victim suspect what is happening to him until the money has been wagered and lost.

Given the knowledge of the key cards in a game, the cardsharp then proceeds to deal them more or less as he wishes. There are two main methods of doing this; both simple, but both almost impossible to detect. One is to deal, not the top card, but the second, third or even fourth card from the top, and yet betray no sign of irregularity in the swift flow of dealing. Similarly, experts can pull any of the first four or five bottom cards to the top and deal them, if that is necessary to their plans.

When the victim deals, the sharper has only knowledge of how the key cards are distributed, but this is enough for him to sometimes win his biggest hauls on a hand he has not dealt himself. When this happens, he can afford to lose quite heavily on his own deal and thus make sure that any suspicion is lulled.

The second main method of marking cards is the "stripper" method. This process involves again much practice and extreme delicacy of touch. The key cards are not marked on the back at all, but merely filed a fraction smaller along their long edges than the unimportant cards. Sometimes this filing, done when the pack is damped on a special frame, does no more than cut a fragile bevelled edge along the master cards—but the irregularity is enough for the cardsharp. His skilled fingers can manipulate the filed cards from top to bottom, from inside to outside the deck, or in the reverse directions, with lightning speed.

Just in "cutting" a deck of already shuffled cards, the crook can arrange to have certain cards dealt to himself—he needs to know the whereabouts of only eight key cards to turn his luck into a certainty. Even if he gets only four of the vital cards, he knows where the others are.

Just as Australians have a reputation as confidence men, so Greeks have the record of being the underworld's best card-sharps. Jo Popoulos, the Greek, as he was known for years in the French and Italian casinos, had an international reputation as an inveterate gambler. But few people knew he was a crook, so cunningly did he disguise his ability to win when he chose. And, like most of the cardsharping gang, Jo was only an indifferent card player in an honest game. Even an average bridge player could have beaten him in an honest deal.

Many crooks cheat without making a mark of any kind on the cards. Their operations have not the limited scope of the marked card experts, whose success depends entirely on playing with doctored cards. These more subtle thieves of the gaming table are the men who work as pairs and disclose their inside knowledge by a system of code signals.

This signalling method can be used by two men playing in a game, or between one man in the game and a spectator. Such partnerships work out a dozen or more different code systems and never use the same system twice in the same club, gambling den or casino.

By the way they place their hands on a match-box, a pencil, their clothing, their faces, the table; by the way they finger their cards as they pick them up and arrange their hands; by the way they speak or blink their eyelids, they can "talk" to each other across a card table as clearly and secretly as if they were passing each other sealed envelopes of instruction and information.

Occasionally they use two systems at once, one to be ignored and the other "official" for the night in question. And some-times, just to make their collusion completely secure from suspicion, they play honestly.

In their "honest" games they win when they can with the

cards they receive from honest dealing. But after the game is finished they meet to split their gains and losses and, in any game of high stakes, one side or the other usually shows a considerable profit.

The art in the "honest" game, lies in urging spectators (kibitzers) or the other members of the game to plunge heavily.

Teams of two, using the code and "honest" system, have been known to operate for years without suffering any risk except the card-player's tendency to surplus weight and smoker's cough.

Such delicate methods, of course, do not yield the quick "kills" that the jugglers of cards achieve; the code men are content to make slow but steady progress and sacrifice the thrill of big hauls for the easy content of a quiet life. On the other hand, they are past masters at arranging games which will yield big rewards.

Not many months ago two American film and stage celebrities visited Britain to perform a series of goodwill shows. They were a big success and their tour earned them something over £20,000 in the course of a few short, but hectic, weeks. Currency restrictions and income tax provisions tied up these quick profits and the visiting stars found they had about £10,000 at their disposal—as long as they spent it in England.

It was easy money and they were both men of the world. They prepared to spend most of it in a bout of relaxation. They had a clear week of doing nothing before they were due to fly back across the Atlantic.

Such ripe plums could hardly go unnoticed, and there were several professional gamblers anxious to get their money, but there were difficulties. The Americans could not be asked to visit one of the many furtive gambling dens that thrive in London without having their suspicions aroused.

There are, however, more ways than one of skinning a cat. Among the many people who exist on the fringe of the theatre was a languid English gentleman who was always short of cash. To eke out his other pickings, he acted as an agent or fixer for two cardsharping partners, both of whom flew to London from France for this special assignment.

They met the impoverished Englishman discreetly at a seedy hotel in Earl's Court and together they worked out the details of their coup.

Within twenty-four hours they were installed in soggy county comfort at the Englishman's family home in Berkshire. And, a couple of days later, the Americans arrived there to experience their first house party in the traditional English manner.

The host was an affable fellow, a little loud in his habits for a typical country squire, but how were the amused Americans to know that. They were entranced by the butler, appalled by the plumbing, and reluctantly impressed by the ancient stone walls of the manor and its emerald sward that carpeted the beech forest surrounding the house. They walked through muddy lanes, jogged black and blue at a local point-to-point meet and toasted before an immense fire in the library.

The host was charming and a man who obviously liked to make a study of his fellow men. The week-end guests were a mixed bag. As well as the Americans there were a wonderful pair of maiden aunts, a crack-pot professor of something from Oxford and a brace of nieces in tweeds who kept telling the Americans they were "terribly amusing". There were also the two Frenchmen—old pals, it was explained, of the host from his days as an artillery major in France before Dunkirk.

The charming Englishman the Americans had met in London was there too in a dim sort of way. But he was hardly noticeable until the last night of their stay because he retired to his bedroom with a bilious attack and did not appear at all until he descended at last and casually suggested a game of cards.

The Americans were a little bored, by this stage, but they were doubtful about playing. They had horrible visions of a game of cribbage, or at best a session of conversational bridge. They could hardly believe their luck when the host suggested the Americans and Frenchmen might care to start a poker game. It had already been made clear to the Americans that the Frenchmen were well-to-do business men.

The Americans lost heavily at first, then picked up. By midnight they were down about £500. The tweedy nieces and the eccentric aunts had gone to bed hours before. The host brought out another bottle of his ancestral Scotch and the poker players really got into their stride. A cosy party by the great log fire.

But there was an air of tension. The Americans were a little impatient; they felt the Frenchmen were closing the game up to make sure of their winnings. After a couple of generous (and beautifully timed) drinks, the Americans suggested they might start taking the game seriously. The Frenchmen were dubious, but the host, who appeared to have drunk a little more than he should have, made a slightly jeering remark about the need for France to have as many American dollars as she could get. Suddenly, the four men were huddled over the cards in deadly earnest.

The setting was perfect, the mood ideal. The Americans lost nearly £11,000 before they gave up. The theatrical friend, who could look upon this night as one of his most successful "productions" was apologetic all the way back to London. He even hinted, in his well-bred way, that the Frenchmen might have been "slightly off-colour cads", but the Americans angrily contradicted this suggestion. They were not complaining. They could cover their losses without any worry. What was all the fuss about.

The Americans left the Englishman when they got back to town and flew home to New York a few hours later. As their plane headed out across the ocean, the Englishman and the French pair met for another farewell to share out the takings—£4,000 each for the visitors from across the Channel and the rest for the whisky-drinking country squire and the Englishman who had brought the Americans into the party.

An elaborate scheme? Perhaps, but a profit of at least £1,000 for having people down for the week-end was not bad for the host. As for the impoverished and charming theatrical agent, his £800 or so was just one of many commissions earned in various settings on the same principle, during the year.

The story demonstrates two things. One is that "face" is almost as important to cardsharps as it is to confidence men. With an appearance of honesty, scheming gamblers can achieve pretty well anything; without it, they cannot even get started in their crooked deals.

The second was the greed of the victims. This greed is as powerful among the very rich gamblers (like King Farouk in his heyday as the playboy of Egypt) as it is among the shabbiest criminals who have a fistful of easy money. In fact many of the experts who make their living at relieving gamblers of their money claim that the wealthier a man is, the more rapacious he becomes at the gaming table. And even when the gambler has lost all his money, his craze for another chance to recoup his fortune is stronger than ever.

Gambling is as much a drug, although it is a mental and not a physical weakness, as heroin. Psychologists have suggested it is a mental illness, a form of obsession and a flight from reality, as serious as any of the recognized nervous disorders.

The hope of winning back all that has been lost, and more, never dies. It becomes so dominating that it has all the strange power of a delusion; the victim is convinced that his luck must change for the better after a run of losses. The cooler brain of mathematicians point out, in vain, that a man's chance of winning on the fall of a card is just as great (and just as remote) each time a new hand is dealt. To have lost fifty times in a row does not necessarily increase the probability that the gambler will do better next time. Each roll of the dice, each deal of the cards offers the same chance of a win or a loss as the others did. Cards and dice have no regard for personalities—unless, of course, the personality is juggling them.

A gambler down on his luck is an ideal tool for unscrupulous crooks. They know such a man will accept any chance to get a little money and try his luck again and it is among these defeated creatures that the cardsharp finds his new recruits when any swindling work is to be done. The thousands of men and women who earn a living bringing in "prospects" to gambling dens and casinos are all of this type. They all dream the same dream—one day they will build their little sums of money into a fortune and escape to happiness.

It never works out that way, for the gambling addict—and gambling is an addiction like any physical drug—cannot fight clear of his weakness. The professional gamblers never try to force their luck. They prefer to make a living out of other people who try to force *their* luck.

The lower grade of professional gambling crooks do not pretend to be subtle in their dealings with the public. They operate in pairs (and sometimes with an attractive woman as a decoy) in hotel bars and lounges, on ships and trains. They pick their simplest of dupes—the country people in town for a spree, drunken spendthrifts and youngsters in search of experience. When a victim is fuddled by drink the cardsharp need hardly bother to go through his tricks.

There is another type of criminal who makes money out of man's weakness for gambling. He is not known as a crook but as a financier, a business man, a manager of big casinos or hotels or lotteries. And he makes more money than even the most expert and presentable cardsharp.

The so-called numbers racket in America meant a take of more than fifteen million dollars a year to the gangsters who ran the business in the early 'thirties. Even now, after several clean-ups by the Federal police, Americans pour twenty-four million dollars a year into the hands of gambling tycoons.

But it is in a country like Brazil, where the daily bet on the numbers of winning lottery tickets is a national pastime, that the biggest operators flourish. The official lotteries provide the basis for *Bishos*, as the side-betting on the lottery results is called, and cities like Sao Paulo have hundreds of shops where a poor man can stake one cruzeiro to win a fortune. The betting shops, all linked to one big syndicate, will accept any bets. The sky is the limit in Bishos and the man who directs this vast, national racket is also a director of big mining concerns, banks and insurance companies.

The Bishos prizes are many and generous. A man can win a fortune by forecasting the winning lottery number or by naming any arrangement of its numerals. The odds against winning are several million to one, but that does not deter the man or woman with a few shillings to invest. Their dream is to collect a fortune for almost nothing, and every day a handful of the millions who make the racket pay *do* collect big sums in prizes. Bishos, the numbers racket in America and the Lotto shops in Malta, all operate on the same principle of mass exploitation of the very human failing of hoping to get something for nothing.

It is an immense field of operation for the man with cunning and no conscience. Whether he extracts his share of the loot by using the *volte* (the cardsharp's trick of flipping the top card to the bottom of the pack with his thumb, under the very noses of his victims) or runs a casino, or controls a national enterprise like the illegal Bishos, the crooked gambler belongs to the same breed.

The cardsharp's friendly face and honest eyes, the casino's deep carpets, bright lights and gracious staff and the Bishos' director's multitude of ticket sellers, are all really the same thing—a front to lull the unwary into the belief that gambling is a mysterious working of the fates which may operate in your favour if you will only give it a chance by playing a hand of cards, staking a little on a spinning wheel or buying a ticket or naming a number.

9
dope and smuggling

DOPE is always in the news. From the ancient trade routes of the Middle East to the swift modern airlines of the American continent there is always a section of the underworld awaiting delivery of a new consignment of "the stuff". To the average man it seems, as he reads his newspapers, that the police of sixty nations are always seizing parcels of heroin, opium, hashish or morphine and arresting the men who carry it. Almost every year the newspapers announce that another drug ring has been broken. Almost every year national health authorities issue grave warnings of the "slow death" in the midst of prosperous communities and say that the drug menace grows stronger each year.

The great, degrading trade in drugs reaches all over the world from Hong Kong and Macao in the East, to Kansas City in the West; from Genoa and the desert trails out of Lebanon in the North, to Singapore and Sourabaya in the South. To the normal citizen it is a vague and horrible world, this secret tide of poison—a no-man's land of perpetual war between the police and smugglers in which neither side seems to win. But to the underworld the drug traffic is the "big time", the golden bonanza of all crime. It brings the biggest profits and has the most powerful gangs. Its directors are ruthless, cunning and enormously wealthy and its thousands of agents (peddlers, carriers, manufacturers and salesmen) are men to whom anything is worth the fat rewards the trade offers them.

Some idea of what the trade *does* offer the various classes of drug traffickers—from the man who sells direct to the customers to the directors of the main source of supply—may be had from the following history of one consignment through its stages from raw material to the consumer.

Opium is the base from which heroin (the favourite form of the drug among Western addicts) is made. It may be grown in

Yugoslavia, China, Turkey, Iran or Mexico, but let us, for the sake of example, take the case of opium grown in Turkey.

Harvesters of the poppy gum (extracted from the growing plants with delicate skill, rather in the way a rubber tapper draws off latex from a rubber tree) treat it by pressing it between poppy leaves until it becomes a blackish-brown thick paste which brings the producer about £2 10s. per lb. on the legal market and £9 or £10 per lb. if he sells to one of the drug rings.

The raw opium base must now be treated in one of the illicit laboratories (many are in Northern Italy) and by the time it is refined to pure heroin its price is £500 a lb. The price for the dope racket buyer in America is £1,000 a lb., plus £250 a lb. for delivery charges.

The original material has already had its value multiplied one hundred times, but the profit margin is just beginning. The wholesale distributors "cut" the pure heroin by mixing it with a chemical powder to one-third of its strength before passing it on to the big distributors with their strings of contact men. By doing this the original lb. of heroin which cost £1,250 or more to get to America is distributed as 3 lbs. of "cut" heroin with a price of £3,750, or £1,250 for 1 lb. of third-strength drug.

Here the contact man steps in with his condensed milk powder and talcum powder to cut the drug still further until it may be only one-eighteenth of its original strength; in this way he gets 6 lbs. of "snow" from each lb. of third-strength heroin. And this diluted powder is sold in small envelopes holding one or two grains of diluted heroin.

There are seven thousand grains in 1 lb. avoirdupois and one grain of the diluted drug is considered enough for one shot for the average addict.

It sells from 10s. to £1 a "shot"—according to the price the consumer is prepared to pay. Assuming each grain of the diluted heroin brings only 10s., the original lb. of pure heroine (now broken up into 18 lbs.) provides 126,000 shots for which the consumers pay at least £63,000. Quite a profit from the original £10 paid for the raw opium base!

To summarize this enormous profit process: the raw material costs £10 a lb.; the processed heroin costs (delivered to the

U.S.) £1,250 a lb.; wholesalers sell this for £3,750; contact men pass it on for £22,500, and the consumers pay £63,000.

These figures are only approximate. Sometimes the margins are bigger, sometimes less—but not often. Only an insatiably hungry market and callously greedy middle-men make such profits possible, but it is easy to see there is ample incentive for the dope traffickers to persevere with their trade despite big risks of heavy penalties and large losses when a consignment is confiscated.

The underworld's drug runners are all specialists in their various branches of the business. They need to be, for the police pitted against them are specialists, too—men who are often called on to play the part of spies in the enemy camp and to risk instant death if they are detected. Human life is of little account in the drug business where there are vast sums of money at stake in the big deals. But there is no lack of men prepared to risk their lives for the sake of the big rewards successful drug trafficking brings.

Other classes of criminal seldom get mixed up in the drug business. They are afraid of the grip the dope gangs get on their agents and also afraid that they might become addicts themselves. European and American recruits to the drug rings come from the adolescent hoodlums who, often without knowing just what they are doing, become runners for distributors. They are carefully selected from among the street gangs.

The roughest and the most daring of the junior criminals are always anxious to attain further social prestige among their fellows. To these youths the patronage of an older man, the running of secret errands and the good money this brings are irresistible baits. Then, having established the youth as a drug delivery boy, the older man makes it clear the boy's errands have put him "in the racket"—and trying to get out is very dangerous. Thus another apprentice is caught in the net.

Gradually he may be promoted in the drug hierarchy from runner to agent with a list of clients; from this, perhaps, to an international courier or a wholesale distributor. Few reach these senior ranks in the drug business. The casualty rate is high; either the police interfere with the youngster's career or some senior member of the narcotic's network decides he is not trustworthy and must be "dumped".

The underworld code of complete secrecy and complete hostility to the police reaches its most complete expression in the dope rings. The slightest suspicion of failure or dishonesty may mean death or a severe beating and an order to "leave town". Fantastic? Not when it is realized what sums of money and what organization are involved, and what risks of ruin every drug peddler runs when something goes wrong.

Only a year ago, for instance, a Turkish ship left Lebanon for Naples. An informer tipped off an American narcotic's sleuth in Rome and the American contacted Interpol. Within hours Interpol had advised the Naples police to search the ship on arrival. They did and found 7,000 lbs. of morphine base, and 39,000 lbs. of raw opium (the material from which heroin is refined).

This illegal cargo was worth more than one million dollars on the Italian drug market. It would have eventually brought up to seven times that amount by the time it was sold to American and European customers. The sort of man at the head of an organization which could finance that shipment is not likely to hesitate if he should come to think that one of his agents is unreliable. In this case, it seemed, someone, somewhere, along the long chain of command from Lebanon to Naples worked off a grudge by informing the police. If the directors of the shipment ever discover the guilty man, there is little doubt that his body will be found sooner or later somewhere along the coastline.

The police will have no lack of places to look for his killer. It might be one of an American group awaiting delivery of part of the cargo; it might be an Italian agent working for the illegal manufacturers of heroin, for whom the Turkish ship was bringing new supplies of raw material; it might be a gunman working for the infuriated "boss" in Lebanon; it might be just another minor operator proving his loyalty to his gang by slaying the traitor. Dozens of criminals are suspected by their drug ring associates whenever there is an accident. Suspicion, greed and ruthless revenge make the drug racket a jungle in which a man either learns to survive quickly or not at all.

The market for illegal dope, in western countries and Europe, is divided into three main classes—very wealthy people who take to drugs as an unusual thrill; stage and film actors and actresses find they cannot maintain the feverish tempo of theatrical life without special stimulants; and American prostitutes, specially those in the "call-girl" racket who are fed "the stuff" to keep them firmly in the grip of their exploiters. There are, of course, thousands of addicts outside these three main classes. Since the war many ex-servicemen have taken to drugs, their nerves and morale shattered by their experiences. And there is a growing number of young people falling into the grip of the drug habit because it is considered "smart" to learn about the illicit pleasures of heroin or marihuana (hashish).

In the Orient and Asia, of course, there has always been a fairly stable percentage of opium smokers, and the Middle East has its hashish addicts. We are not concerned with the methods of taking these drugs, nor with the complete physical and mental rot they cause as habit becomes addiction and addiction a disease that knows no relief. But it is well to mention that very few addicts succeed in freeing themselves from drugs. It takes enormous will-power and sustained courage to endure the physical tortures of deprivation and—even then—there is no guarantee that the craving may not return at any time.

What is more within the scope of this survey of underworld workings is a consideration of the routes of supply and the methods of manufacture and distribution.

Drug trafficking, more than any other illegal activity, involves international organization. The best way to illustrate this is probably to attempt to trace the origin of the few grains of heroin some unfortunate New Yorker buys furtively from a distributor on a street corner, or collects while pretending to have a cup of coffee with "a friend" in a cafe.

The man from whom addicts get "the stuff" is the lowest of the drug traffic's workers—a runner (in New York district large numbers of these peddlers are Porto Ricans). He collects fifty or a hundred dollars from the customer and takes it back to the local agent. A local agent has a list of clients, maybe fifty or so, whom he knows by sight and has accepted only on recommendation from other customers. Even local agents, about as important in the drug traffic as a newspaper seller is in the newspaper industry, must always be on the look-out for police spies and wary of informers. The local agent pays his runner well for each delivery, probably ten dollars. He can afford to do this. Every man handling illegal drugs works on a handsome margin of profit and knows he must pay as lavishly as he gets paid himself.

The local agents get their supplies from a "contact" generally a prosperous minor gangster. But agents seldom collect direct from the contact; they pick their drugs up from a store, or a railway station parcels office—and always pay before collecting. (The receiver of drugs at all stages in the game must pay first and trust his supplier not to cheat him. The nearer we come to the initial source of supply, quantities handled are larger and the temptation to swindle grows greater).

The contact gets his supplies from one of the many central depots or gang hide-outs. Here the imported drug is "cut" (i.e. diluted) to as little as one-hundredth of its imported strength. The contact man picks his drugs up from agents of the central depot. These agents never do business unaccompanied "in case there is trouble".

The depots cut the drugs, generally by mixing them with talcum powder or condensed milk powder, and receive their supplies from smugglers' agents. These operatives are key men. They may gather their supplies from drug-running seamen, pick them up off-shore in specially wrapped, buoyant packets or collect them from air-travelling couriers. All the tricks of smuggling come into play at this stage of the business. False-bottomed luggage, cans and packets of food in which heroin or opium has been inserted before export; rubber tubes carried inside the body and every ingenious disguise from toothpaste to children's toys is used to defeat the customs and police.

The seamen and other smugglers who carry small amounts (1 lb. of pure heroin commands about 5,000 dollars at this stage of the process) are carefully selected by the exporters of the illegal drugs and earn big money for their part in the distribution of bulk supplies.

Tracing the envelope of "snow" bought in a New York cafe (where the drug is sold for about two dollars a grain) back to its original source now takes us a big step up in the drug traffic caste-system. So far we have discussed only the retailers, the delivery boys, the importers and carriers of the drugs. Now we come to the bulk manufacturers, a shadowy tribe whose names are seldom exposed and whose identity is as carefully guarded from the underworld as it is from the forces of the law.

The north of Italy is the centre of the world's heroin traffic. Milan and Turin are the two main Italian centres for the manufacture of medicinal drugs where, under lawful licence, big laboratories are permitted to make 330 lb. of pure heroin per year. But, in one recent year, Italian and international police agents calculated that 770 lbs. of the drug were made and smuggled out of the country to other parts of Europe and America!

The main export port for illegal drugs is Genoa and the chief port for importation of the raw materials is Trieste, where shipments of hashish and opium pour in from Turkey, Greece and Yugoslavia. The drug ring experts who work near the main supply system for world dope are men who never appear in the courts of the world as dope traffickers. They must have big resources of men and money. They operate as financiers and directors of the trade.

But the crooks of dozens of seaport cities, hundreds of seamen (from humble sailors to masters and owners of the Mediterranean's immense fleet of small boats and ships) and the scum of hundreds of towns along the desert fringe of North Africa, Egypt, Palestine and Lebanon provide the men for the front-line of the drug traffic. They are often desperate men, inured to a life of violence and quite prepared to shoot it out with anti-narcotics police of their own rival gangs in the trade when a crisis develops.

The men who arrange the big deals, which are the basis of the drug traffic, deal through intermediaries in Beirut, Genoa, Naples, Rome, Algiers, Singapore, New York and New Orleans, Paris and Marseilles. No one director of the trade, of course, has contacts in more than two or three of these centres, but the drug network, taken in its overall strength, reaches to every corner of the earth. The big deals are organized through coded cable messages or, more generally, by word-of-mouth agents and couriers with sealed instructions to be delivered to a contact in another country.

It is a strange ever-changing pattern in which every man tries to cover up his part in the transaction and, should an individual be trapped by the police, he can tell tnem nothing except "a stranger gave me a packet to hand to a man I've never seen before". This time-worn denial is the standard statment of all drug ring operatives whether they are apprehended stepping from a plane at London airport or seized trying to cross a frontier post between Trans-Jordan and Palestine on the desert run from Lebanon to Egypt by camel caravan. One courier will have his money or his drugs concealed between the sides of a luxury pigskin attache case, another will be carrying hashish at the bottom of a laundry basket crammed with soiled rags—but both are doing the same job for the same reason.

The drug traffic, despite the huge amounts of money involved in its transactions, is little more than a prolonged gamble for many of its operatives. An agent trusted, say, with a packet of pure heroin for delivery in Kansas City (one of the big distribution and "cutting" centres in the United States) may meet a man in Paris who is prepared to pay a higher price than the one arranged between the agent's principals. If he thinks he can get away with it, the agent sells his secret cargo to the highest bidder and disappears. The purchaser of the consignment, who has paid in advance for the drug, is left lamenting.

Or a swindle can be worked another way. An agent delivering drugs nearly always does so in conditions of furtive secrecy. A meeting in a car is often arranged where the drug is passed from agent to buyer and the money collected on the spot. Both parties generally bring companions with them to make sure the deal goes through smoothly. But the money may be counterfeit, or the drug may be "cut" to a tenth of its claimed quality. This atmosphere of double-dealing is accepted by most gangs as inevitable in their ruthless trade where any trick is justified by a quick clean-up if the chances of pulling it off are at all reasonable.

But the traffic goes on steadily. Only a small percentage of deals are crooked between the men involved at the higher levels of organization. No business can run without trust and the drug traffic is as dependent on good faith in oral agreement as any legitimate enterprise.

What makes the narcotics trade such a hazardous one is that

almost every delivery of a drug is also a complete sale from carrier to receiver. Once away from the big operators, the drug handlers are faced with constant temptation to swindle—a temptation held in check only by fear of reprisal.

There is another factor running through all the transactions of the drug trade and that is the ever-present suspicion that any man may be a police spy. Police in nearly every country fighting the narcotic menace are agreed that the best, indeed the only, way to secure a conviction against the drug-peddlers is to pretend to be in the racket.

American Narcotic Bureau staff often have themselves gaoled with dope ring suspects and assigned to the same cell. Here, in the intimacy of prison and armed with a knowledge of the main characters involved in the particular dope gang, a policeman has a fair chance of being accepted as another crook. Once he has gained a drug-runner's confidence (by no means an easy task) the police agent then hopes to become involved in a deal so that he may catch at least two of the criminals in the act of handling "the stuff".

One big U.S.-Italian syndicate was revealed in this way about three years ago when a crook, enraged by being double-crossed in a big deal, turned informer and knowingly allowed a detective to get into a series of drug negotiations between a group in Naples and a Harlem mob. The policeman might have secured many convictions, but, when he was almost ready to act, the Harlem gang got wind of the trap and the informer was murdered in an East Side cafe. Months of patient and dangerous work thus went for nothing.

The Mafia, the secret Sicilian crime society, is ideally designed to handle drug deals. The Mafia has a system of enforced loyalty to its groups which no ordinary gang can hope to equal.

It is generally recognized that some of the biggest dope rings now operating between Italy and America are dominated by Mafia members. Police have little difficulty in catching a proportion of drug operators on the lower levels of the traffic, but the problem of collecting evidence that will put the senior drug-traffickers behind bars seems almost insurmountable.

The big men are so often wealthy and, apart from their secret interest in narcotics, eminently respectable citizens.

They provide the money, supply influence in high quarters and have contacts among government departments and big pharmaceutical firms that no gangster could hope to enjoy. They draw huge dividends for making the drug traffic possible by putting the criminal element in touch with the source of supply. Then they wash their hands of the whole dirty business and let the crooks get on with the practical and dangerous details of distribution and sale.

The dope smuggling business is, without doubt, the most sordid and distasteful trade in the underworld, with the possible exception of the brothel racket. Let us take a close look at a typical drug-peddler—the man who sells direct to the consumer—and examine a routine day in his working life. He is a man, remember, who is prepared to trade in poison for the sake of making what he thinks is an easy living. Perhaps he averages £100 per week and it might seem to many people that this glamour wage is sufficient reward for the risks he takes.

In appearance our typical dope operator can be anything. He is indistinguishable from the usual run of loungers around the bars and coffee shops of any big city. He spends a lot of money on clothes. His suits are cut in the current "smart guy" fashion and made of the best imported cloth. His shoes are hand made. He spends freely on his own creature comforts—he dines well and tips heavily. All the vulgar graces are his and nearly everything he does is designed to impress the world with his wealth. His women, like his clothes, are the best that money can buy.

There is one distinguishing characteristic, however. He is always on guard. Other criminals can afford to relax when they are among friends, but the drug-peddler is always watchful. He can trust no one and expects no one to trust him. Although he may give the impression of tough self-possession, his eyes scan every new arrival in a cafe, assess every customer in a bar, wherever he may be. His day runs to a set pattern as rigidly governed by the need to earn a living as any of the wage-plugs the drug-peddler scorns.

He must contact his "runners" at perhaps half a dozen different points in his neighbourhood and give them their packets of "snow" for delivery. He is always having to check on their honesty to make sure they are not keeping some of the money they collect for themselves and he is always prepared to discover that some difficulty has arisen with the police. Somewhere along the line someone is always ready to squeeze a little more from the drug-peddler. He is a most vulnerable crook for the parasites of the criminal community and the bigger and better his distribution system is the more chances does it give for the minor blackmail he has to pay.

These are his problems as a distributor to regular clients. But he must always be drumming up new business. Drug addicts are a restless lot, they are always moving on from one district to another and peddlers must be ever on the look-out for new victims. The dope-peddler's days are spent in bars, cafes and pool-rooms and every time a new client approaches him the peddler must check and double-check. He has to sell just one packet of dope to a police spy and his laboriously constructed market is destroyed—by the time he gets out of prison he must start all over again.

There is also the problem of supply. This is always an unpredictable business. Contacts in this field change a lot and "accidents" are frequent. A man, previously dependable, may suddenly claim that no stocks are available or, if they can be procured, that the price is higher than it was last week. The pedlar cannot afford to argue. His whole prosperity depends on maintaining a regular flow of dope to his safe and approved customers.

He is also afraid to argue. The contact men providing the bulk supplies are real gangsters with only one reaction to an agent who, in their opinion, becomes difficult. They either beat him up or turn him over to the police.

The dope-peddler works a long day. He must be prepared to keep appointments with the senior members of the racket at any hour of the day or night, to wait patiently without complaint and, at all costs, to keep his mouth shut no matter what grievance he may have. His success depends on being regarded favourably by the contact men and he knows that, at any time, he can be discarded in favour of another man who is prepared to pay a higher price or who, for some reason, is more acceptable to the agents supplying the drugs. There is also a constant dread of becoming suspect as an informer. There is no chance of argument or appeal when this happens. There are only two courses of action—get out of town or accept a last appointment with the contact men and take what comes philosophically.

Fine clothes, brassy girls and gambling are all the drug-peddler can buy with his profits. They would be enough to keep him happy if only he could feel secure in his prosperity. He has no moral qualms about the trade he is in. If people are silly enough to buy dope, he argues, that is their affair. There is nothing worse about selling drugs to rot customers' lives than there is for a sweet seller to sell sweets to rot people's teeth. With luck the pedlar may graduate a little further up the dope ladder to become a bulk distributor and then his petty fears are replaced by larger ones. The more he knows, the more careful he must be never to become suspect.

It is not surprising that other types of criminal prefer to keep clear of the dope racket. They, at least, know where their enemies lie and can enjoy a measure of confidence among their fellow crooks. The dope racketeers recruit their beginners while they are young, as we have already explained, and once a man is involved in the drug business he bars himself from other departments of crime. To succeed he must become a super-thug and endure a life of perpetual distrust.

Any man of intelligence, even if a law-breaker, can see the traps in the drug racket and fights shy of them. The dope experts are essentially immature mentally and their lives are ruled by fear. Easy money? It would seem to be the hardest earned money in the world, but the tragedy is that so many are tempted into the dirtiest trade on earth.

We have been discussing a typical dope-peddler in a big city, a rank and file member of the international dope rings. But these creatures are not more numerous than the smugglers who keep the supplies of opium, heroin and hashish moving across the face of the earth. In recent years the overall pattern of supply has altered greatly.

Following the revolution in China the main supply of opium has been cut off, or, at least changed. The old links that brought opium from the East through Singapore and Indonesia have altered. Communist China, it is reported, maintains a big flow of raw opium to the "decadent" foreign countries but in effect these supplies are channelled to the many scattered overseas Chinese communities through South East Asia.

The main outlet for opium now is through Macao and the suppliers are, it is claimed, no longer private traders but government officials whose task it is to earn dollar and sterling resources for the new China. Thousands of small craft, from old junks to fast motor-cruisers (remnants of war-time naval disposals of surplus vessels) work the China coast and the long line of Indo-China ports from Hanoi south to Saigon, as well as the big shipping centres of Singapore. It is not difficult for drug smugglers to filter their cargoes through the customs and police barriers in this vast area. From these ports the drug rings use sailors of every nationality in the ships that sail to all points of the western world.

Despite the elaborate precautions that accompany the customs clearance of big ships in modern ports, the detection of small parcels of drugs is immensely difficult. Experienced seamen smugglers do not attempt to unload their contraband until the formal clearance of the ship is completed and, unless the authorities have been told that a certain ship is carrying hidden drugs, a complete search is not attempted. Parcels of drugs can either be dropped overboard at pre-arranged points near the entrance to harbours (and picked up by shore-based operators) or be carried ashore in cargo or by the seamen themselves. Garbage pails, laundry hampers, personal luggage, crates, machinery and tools all provide a cover for drug smuggling and, should an individual be caught, police get nothing more than the standard reply to their questions: "The stuff was picked up from a stranger to be handed over to an unknown party."

In the Middle East the drug tide carries not opium, but hashish. Here again the vast and scruffy sea-going traffic of dhows that wanders along the coast-line of the Red Sea is the vehicle for the main flow of illicit cargo. Ashore it travels by camel caravan along lonely desert trade routes as old as commerce. The opium base and hashish drifts south from Turkey and Yugoslavia around the eastern end of the Mediterranean and over the territory now known as Israel—the oldest land bridge for East-West trade in the world. Many drug traffickers have their headquarters in Lebanon. They are the big financers who buy the raw materials and send them on to the manufacturers in Italy before the refined dope starts its furtive journey into Europe and America.

The dope does not travel without difficulty. Police of every nation along the route are always harrassing the smugglers and a recent case, reported by an Inspector J. L. Kaufman, of the Israel Police, is typical of the running war between the dope racket and the legal forces of the world. Israel police managed to work one of their staff into a group of smugglers by having the policeman pose as a drug-peddler. He arranged to pick up a parcel of hashish with a smuggler and, by hailing a taxi driven by another police agent (and with a third policeman concealed in the luggage boot) he was well on the way to catching his suspects red-handed.

He had taken a further precaution, not knowing how many smugglers he would encounter at the rendezvous. As the taxi was leaving the town, a traffic inspector pulled it up and pretended to make out a speeding charge against the driver. During this conversation the traffic policeman managed to discover where the taxi was headed and, when a following car of police came along, the traffic cop was able to direct them to the rendezvous. This had not been revealed until the police spy entered the car.

At the point of sale, a cave in a patch of deserted hilly country outside the city, the concealed policeman leaped from the boot of the car and, together with the taxi driver and the fake smuggler, tried to arrest the startled drug men. A fierce struggle developed and only the arrival of the following police car enabled the narcotics squad to arrest their men.

If the drug route is not taken overland, either through or skirting the desert borders of Israel to Egypt, it travels by sea along the coast in small ships and sailing boats. Egypt and the other Arab countries of North Africa provide the main market for hashish, but most of the opium base goes to Italy or France for refining into heroin, morphine or codeine.

The dope smugglers are nothing more than gangsters who attain what organization and control they have over their agents by violence and threats of violence. They are a vast, callous tribe of thugs living on the diseased cravings of addicts. They have little subtlety in their methods which seldom arise above blackmail, bribery and murder, but they do operate to a vast extent and, although individuals are often caught, the chain of command is so well protected by the traffic's code of denial of all charges that the really important operators are never revealed.

Smugglers of other goods, particularly of diamonds, gold, currency and strategic metals operate by entirely different methods. The rewards for this type of dealing are often as great as in the drug traffic, but the men operating in this field must have qualifications, ability and resources the dope racketeers know nothing about.

Professional smugglers of precious stones, currency and scarce raw materials are essentially business men as well as crooks. They must understand their markets, both as buyers and sellers, just as thoroughly as any orthodox dealer. They know where and when shortages of any commodity are likely to occur and they must prepare their organizations to exploit the situation before it arises. These men never use violence. Such crudity is as foreign to their manner of doing business as it would be for a city financier dealing in stocks and shares.

These merchants operate with an added margin of profit—the margin for dishonesty and cunning that a normal business man never contemplates seriously but would often love to share as he dutifully pays customs duty and sales tax and obeys all the restrictive orders modern governments impose from time to time to help balance their international trading accounts. The margin provided by dodging customs, sales tax (and, of course, income and company taxes on deals that never get declared because they are illegal) can be a big one. But even when the customs levy amounts to only five or six per cent big operators can make additional thousands by taking a little extra trouble and big risks.

Since the war and during the uneasy years of small conflicts at various parts of the globe, the trading smuggler has had a wide open field. Shortages in Europe took years to overcome and, although most of the commodity gaps are now filled, there are still many goods in short supply in areas where traders are prepared to pay inflated prices and not ask too many questions about the origin of their shipments. The great boom in diamonds is more or less over now (there is, however, a permanent dividend to be won by smuggling first-class stones) and the same easing has occurred in the international gold smuggling racket. But there are still big black-market demands for special minerals used in the hardening of light metals, for copper, industrial diamonds, rubber and other strategic materials.

The men who deal in these markets and, earlier, the diamond and gold markets, operate on a huge scale. This means they must have tens of thousands of pounds available to carry stocks, to make arrangements for shipments, to buy off officials where they can be bribed and to absorb the losses that occur when something goes wrong and a consignment of considerable value is confiscated by the authorities or high-jacked by thieves. (As in all underworld enterprises, the danger of information leaking is ever-present. The basic principle that it is easier to rob a crook than an honest man applies with particular force with smuggling victims. They do not run for the police.)

The smugglers must, of course, have considerable contacts with many of the underworld's experts—the forgers of official documents, receivers and the essential adventurers who are prepared to work outside the law and take the blame if anything goes wrong. The rewards they demand for working for big money operators are high and the smugglers are in no position to haggle over the fees they pay for the physical movement of the goods they juggle around the world.

Perhaps one of the most important and highly developed skills professional smugglers develop is the art of telling whether a man is honest. This term might seem a little out of place in this context of underworld cunning, but dependability and loyalty are essential attributes in a smuggler's agent when the goods being carried are worth, sometimes, hundreds of thousands of pounds. To have well-laid plans and big investments ruined by some carelessness or individual greed is too great a risk. The checking and testing of suitable operatives in the illegal shipment of valuable commodities has become a little known science among the men whose business it is to beat the law for a living without acquiring a criminal record themselves.

The professional speculators in diamonds or currency are skilled traders who seldom embark on a gamble. They know the exact price they can raise for any shipment in a dozen different markets. They carefully weigh the risks of detection against the profits to be made by taking those risks and, when they are ready to act, they must move surely and swiftly. The delay of a day or so can change a deal in currency from profit to heavy loss, just as it does in ordinary commerce in these fields but for the smuggler there is always the added risk of detention.

The directors of smuggling at these top levels of underworld enterprises must be highly presentable men, capable of maintaining the same social status and business standing as the most prosperous and solid honest traders. Their greatest defence is their unassailable appearance of integrity and dignified solvency. It is by mixing in legitimate circles of industry and finance that they glean their working knowledge of the black markets, learn the procedures and limitations of orthodox dealing and devise ways of getting around them.

Many of these avenues for dishonesty involve specialized technical knowledge of interest only to those involved in the particular trade, but there is one department of inquiry which every layman who has crossed a frontier or entered a foreign country by ship or plane will readily appreciate.

In some countries foreigners may wait in public lounges after their immigration check has been completed and before they have had their luggage cleared by customs. This provides an ideal opportunity to unload contraband. In some customs checks, officials pick up every case and parcel to make sure its weight corresponds, within reasonable limits, to its bulk. It is surprising how often this elementary check is either overlooked or neglected.

By sending observers through various routes on trial runs, the smuggler acquires a detailed knowledge of customs routine wherever he plans to operate and can pick their weaknesses. He learns where a minute or so of unguarded time may be used to pass his contraband, where certain officials are "approachable" and how they may be approached and what the element of risk of complete search is in each place his couriers will use.

The couriers themselves, of course, build up a valuable knowledge in this field and different men have different preferences for the routes they work. They seldom travel the same way more than three times, and these are widely spaced trips to avoid the possibility of their faces becoming even vaguely familiar to the officials. "Honest" couriers (i.e. dependable as far as the smuggler is concerned) must have a solid front of respectability and comfortable means. There is a nice matter of judgment in deciding whether a man looks prosperous enough, and not too prosperous, for this type of work.

The veteran in the smuggling business can make a very shrewd guess at a man's, or woman's, honesty in two ways. One is by doing a little business with him on a small scale and seeing to it that the recruit gets a chance to cheat. Perhaps a man will be sent from London to Paris with a small packet of diamonds for which he is told he will be paid £2,000. The contact who meets him will offer, perhaps, £2,200. If the courier tries to keep the extra money for himself he will be considered unsuitable; that is all. There will be no violence, not even any denunciation of the swindler's action. But such dishonesty is not forgotten and the underworld is a smaller place than the world—the two parties might well meet again and the cheat is likely to live to regret his indiscretion.

In the big deals, of course, transactions such as this do not take place. Cash payments are reserved for the small-scale smugglers. The big men operate on an international credit system in which funds built up in almost any country are valuable for future deals and moneys due are deducted in the course of other business when the seller becomes a buyer.

The other way to gauge a prospective courier's character is to play cards with him. Experienced men can tell, after an hour or two at the card table, just where a stranger's weaknesses lie. They can pick the greedy man, the timid man, the vain and over-confident character, and the type who tends to panic when the tension is high. The man under inspection on these occasions does not suspect, of course, that his card-playing is a test. Such games are arranged on a casual basis and often the prospect and his potential employer have never met before—and never meet again.

Apart from the couriers hired as professional experts in deceiving the customs, there is a numerous class of amateur smugglers who, because of their diplomatic or service rank, have certain privileges and advantages when it comes to passing from one country to another. Minor diplomatic officials (even senior ones among the embassy staffs of smaller countries) and air force and army personnel are often surprisingly "available" to a smuggler who knows how to handle matters with discretion.

In post-war Europe with thousands of service and diplomatic officials shuttling to and fro on missions of aid and international co-operation, it was not difficult to discover people who were prepared to deliver packets for a fee. Sometimes the fee rose as high as £3,000 (for a South American ambassador with his own car) but normally £1,000 would buy an attache or a fairly high-ranking officer who was asked to do nothing but hand a package over to an unobtrusive stranger.

Seasoned smugglers and their trusted agents approach a customs clearance with cheerful confidence. They have learned that, unless a tip has been passed to the officials, they have nothing to fear from a normal check. And if a word has been given to the officials, there is nothing to be done about it but stay calm and deny everything. Operating on this basis cuts the nervous strain to a minimum. A professional smuggler considers he has to be terribly unlucky to be caught. He knows this occupational hazard is far less in smuggling at the high level than in any other branch of crime.

The practical tricks of smuggling are not as important to the big operators as their basic cover of presenting a front of respectability, but they do, on occasions, use most of the ruses so popular in fiction. It is not difficult to hide £50,000 worth of diamonds in a partly used tube of toothpaste or the high heels of a woman's shoes. (There was a case a few years ago, when a man and a woman travelling together were found to have one and a half million dollars worth of diamonds in their collective heels as they entered New York from the Continent. They were detected, not by routine inspection, but during a special check which could have occurred only because someone had leaked information to the police.

For currency smuggling and gold bars, the false "bunkers" (hollow compartments) built into the boots of tourists' cars are often used. Some gold smugglers have even had their bumper bars made of gold and chromed to make them appear normal; but this device is not only elaborate but dangerous. Too many people must know of the trick by the time the bars have been made and fitted, to make it safe enough for the cautious tastes of the established professionals. Every man who knows something of a big smuggling deal is a risk to the operation. The bigger the operation, the fewer the collaborators the better. Hollowed brush handles, false bottoms in trunks, dummy ribs on cases, and the secret filling of handrails on planes and trains on the Continent are among the devices that have been, and are still, used successfully. But all of these tricks are of little use if the deal becomes suspect. Once that happens the officials have the suspect more or less cornered. X-ray checks reveal almost any hidden cargo and the customs searchers are well versed in the cunning of hiding contraband.

Professional smugglers in the top brackets in the business know little of these methods. They are brokers dealing in illegal futures rather than merchants or distributors of the goods they handle. The vast fortunes made from smuggled watches in Europe were made by the men who financed and organized the wholesale markets, not by the far more colourful characters who shipped them and, once they were landed in their country of destination, distributed them furtively to the retailers. These are expert, but definitely more ordinary skills as far as the directors of the illegal exports and imports are concerned.

Indeed they tend to look down on the practical smugglers like those that scuttle to and fro across the Mediterranean with cigarettes, nylons and other scarce supplies from the free port of Algiers and the merchant ships which see fit to unload parts of their cargoes to smugglers on the high seas. This highly risky trade, the temptation and downfall of many an amateur crook, does not attract either the big professionals or the lower criminal element of the underworld. The big men hate risks almost as much as bankers do and the tougher, more primitive crooks prefer to extract their share from such smuggling by waiting until the goods are ashore and then stealing them.

The men operating in this theatre of smuggling operations are mainly ex-servicemen, who saw the opportunities during their war-time duties in North Africa, Sicily and Italy and came back as civilians to clean up a quick fortune and retire. Many of them succeeded, but the business tailed off rapidly as normal international trade was restored. Also heavy penalties gradually deterred the local crooks from handling contraband material in their own countries. They became known to the police and, consequently, fairly easy to apprehend.

At one stage almost any man who could handle a boat could operate at a handsome profit between Algiers and the coasts of Spain, France and Italy. These were the men who most nearly approached the smugglers of history, the rugged, colourful seafarers with caves in cliffs and almost a sporting affection for their enemies, the excise men. But there is more to be made than the difference between duty-paid and duty-free goods when shortages ashore create an inflated price as well. As the shortages dwindle, the game becomes hardly worth the candle.

There is a final class of smuggler, a professional who devotes a life time to this form of crime. This group is made up of the inhabitants of border towns and villages through Europe who have made petty smuggling a feature of frontier life for centuries. These humble operators, who play a constant game of hide-and-seek with their many equivalents of the village policeman, have few contacts with the organized aspects of the underworld. Their role, in recent years, however, has given them a new importance because the goods they have been smuggling have come to include people—desperate and pathetic victims of national tensions and international political trends.

The men and women who have accepted risks of smuggling liquor, tobacco and food across frontiers as part of every-day existence for generations have proved not only expert, but highly courageous in outwitting the border controls of humanity between Iron Curtain territories and the rest of Europe. The prices they charge are often high, but the risks of detection are greater and the punishments infinitely more drastic than they have ever been.

Perhaps the closest link these border smugglers have with the rest of the world of crime is that from their ranks come many of the recruits of the pickpocket fraternity. These beginners learn the basic skills of their trade in country towns where there is an atmosphere of constant opposition to the police and frontier guards. This early experience in outwitting the law is a most important factor in the breeding of criminals. By the time a boy smuggler or pickpocket is grown to manhood he finds the underworld an easier and more natural place to live in than the lawful community to which, fortunately, the great majority of mankind belong.

Dope traffickers, diamond smugglers, and all the lesser classes of cheats in international crime are, by mature adult standards, defeated personalities who have not been able to cope with the rules and regulations of normal life. But it is not always easy to define the frontier between the world and the underworld. A diamond dealer, operating a legitimate business, who offers an innocent seller £500 for a stone an expert knows to be worth three times that price, is not a crook in the eyes of the law—he is just a hard business man.

If the deal goes through, however, it is hard to see why the dealer should not be regarded as a thief who has taken £1,000 from a defenceless victim; nor why he should be looked upon any more tolerantly than the smuggler who swindles the State out of £1,000 worth of customs dues. Indeed, it can be argued, that the "business man" is an even less likeable fellow than the smuggler who after all accepts considerable risks to make his living dishonestly.

The underworld, in its more expert sections, such as those where the smuggler, the confidence man and the counterfeiter and forger operate, is not very far removed from the shadier grades of sharp practice in the legal world of commercial enterprise; or so it seems to many of the underworld community.

10
counterfeiters and forgers

NEXT to dope smuggling, counterfeiting is the greatest of the rackets in crime. This fabulous kingdom of counterfeit has as many variations in method, both of production and distribution, as it has operators. From the big gangs, which plan currency frauds running into millions, to the eccentric lone operators who pass one faked note a time, the counterfeiter provides an observer of the underworld with a fascinating variety of human nature on the wrong side of the law.

The big counterfeit organizations employ all types of people, from the essential artists, who copy the notes or coins to be faked, to the large teams of distributors and the little teams of thugs who stand by ready to use force if it is needed. The draughtsman working on the printing plates, photographic negatives and the actual counterfeit notes are all as skilled as any craftsmen earning an honest living by their art. There are occasions when the counterfeiter is acknowledged to be better than most honest tradesmen.

What makes such gifted men turn their talents to crime when they could earn good money in orthodox ways? The answers to this question are as different as the personalities involved. The basic reason, of course, is greed and reluctance to work for a living, but there are many shades of motive apart from these. Some of the cleverest counterfeiters derive an intense, if perverted, satisfaction from fooling the banks. Some develop a compulsion to make up for frustrations and disappointments in their lives, by cheating.

The artistic temperament is a rich field for the psychologist and the student of human behaviour generally. In the field of crime, one often finds an added quirk of oddity that has driven an otherwise intelligent and capable craftsman into the uneasy secrecy of illegal skills.

Counterfeiters suffer from a strange contradiction of the

normal artist's liking, and even need, for recognition. The counterfeiter may never have this healthy and conventional satisfaction. The more successful he is, the greater does his inner sense of frustration as an artist become. His criminal associates, who exploit his talent, are incapable of appreciating the quality of the work he does—apart from assessing how easy it will be to distribute. Many counterfeiters are not interested in this sort of admiration. They have two conflicting desires—to work out a revenge against society in secret by robbing it, and to be hailed as brilliant technicians and artists. But the people who know their work cannot appreciate it as art; and the people who might appreciate it in this way must never know about it. In many instances a counterfeiter's greatest hour of achievement (although it is ironical victory) is when he is arrested, tried in public and branded as master crook. It is then, and only then, that he attains the recognition he has yearned for so long in secret and yet, perhaps, never admitted even to himself.

The modern counterfeiter, with his photographic and chemcal processes for imitating currency, is often superbly skilled and does a convincing job. But the men who operated fifty years ago and earlier were the masters of an art. Their success depended on microscopic accuracy in the infinitely delicate engraving and draughtsmanship without any mechanical aids. Some of the talented counterfeiters of the past were penmen and artists of world standing, or would have been had they used their skill honestly.

Many forgers enter their trade without meaning to do so. A man who countersigns his boss's signature and then uses it on some unimportant document may find he is sent to goal—and it is here that his talent is suddenly exploited on a professional basis. The amateur forger learns dozens of new tricks from his criminal associates in gaol and, when he is released, underworld contacts are waiting for him with a job. As he is barred from respectable employment, he is an easy prey. Many banknote forgery jobs are planned in prison.

The underworld's artists in counterfeiting are by no means limited to faking currency and coin. They can make passports, share scrip, bonds, visa stamps, travellers' cheques, documents of identity of all descriptions, legal agreements, seals and sometimes work at imitating paintings, sculpture and china. They are essential to many branches of the underworld, for there is always an illegal demand for fake money, forged passports and documents of identity among the restless drift of crooks on the run, or among smugglers, confidence men and pickpockets who must spread their activities to remain in business.

One of the most profitable forging trades is that of counterfeiting travellers' cheques. These are often stolen by pickpockets and brought to the forgers so that they may be used. It is a highly specialized branch of the business and is, in a sense, a subdivision of the receiver's trade. Many receivers of stolen property do nothing else but buy up travellers' cheques and then cash them by having forgers imitate the signatures of the owners.

More ambitious use of travellers' cheques is made by the organized groups. These gangs are divided into business and craft sections. The business department is responsible for acquiring the correct paper and plant for printing, and the artists do the counterfeiting. When this is done, cleverly organized teams of distributors unload them in various markets —particularly among other crooks.

Thieves are another source of big business for the forgers and counterfeiters. They bring in bonds and shares, receipt forms and other documents which can be reproduced and used to great advantage by the great army of confidence men who prey continually on the gullible (and greedy) public.

Perhaps the most gullible customers are the collectors and art buyers who have not only greed, but the consuming passion of snobbery to cloud their judgment in their desire to own exclusive posessions. (See *Confidence men*; and points made later in this chapter).

Another busy section of the trade is in passports. To the expert, these are relatively easy to counterfeit, amend or forge. This is true even now, although before the war when international barriers were less difficult to pass, it was much easier. Scandinavian passports were then the favourite purchase among European and American crooks as they needed no visas. These days many countries have made their passports difficult, but not impossible, to reproduce illegally.

Special papers, embossed stamps, fingerprints imposed over both photograph of the holder and the holder's signature and more elaborate printing have posed the forgers and counterfeiters with new problems. But stolen passports can be doctored in many ways to serve another user. Washing techniques, the repair of damaged paper surfaces with carefully applied white of egg, special inks and, always, brilliant draughtsmanship can overcome nearly all the protective devices which customs and other officials have introduced.

Unless police are really searching for a crook, he has an excellent chance of moving about with forged papers. Most customs officials take only a cursory glance at passports and the crooks know there is no risk involved—unless the authorities are making a special check for him. Even this risk is of little moment in a criminal's existence. He accepts far greater chances of detection as normal hazards in the course of his every-day operations. The average honest citizen trying to bring home a bottle of undeclared perfume is far more likely to give himself away by nervous anxiety than the professional travelling on a forged passport with a few thousand pounds worth of smuggled goods or currency in his luggage.

The coin counterfeiters are not as numerous as the paper currency experts because their equipment, which must include a heavy forging press, is necessarily more cumbersome and difficult to conceal. Their profits are also lower on each article, but, once established, they sometimes make up in quantity what they lose in the value of each counterfeited product. Europe's currency always contains a considerable proportion of counterfeit coin and many of the Middle East and Asian countries provide richly rewarding markets for the coin-makers.

White Russians in China used to make big quantities of silver dollars, but this profitable trade ended when the Chiang Kai-shek regime collapsed and the counterfeiters had to split up and travel to other countries.

Big shipments of spurious coins are unloaded in North Africa, Egypt and some of the Arab countries by counterfeit rings with networks almost as elaborate and far-flung as those in the dope racket. The makers sell their product for about ninety per cent of its purported face value to the big dealers, who make a handsome profit as they deal in large quantities. Many somewhat crude coins are made and passed by the local eccentrics in communities all over the world, some counterfeiters even finding it profitable to make two shilling or one shilling pieces for the sake of a little easy money. Small-value coins have the attraction of being easy to pass, but no professional counterfeiter will bother with them.

Sovereigns, made in many European countries, provide an interesting example of how time and changing habits can open up a field for the underworld's enterprising technicians. The fake sovereigns are excellently made and contain the statutory quantity of gold (123.27447 grains), but they sell for more than the price of their gold content, particularly in the Far East where gold coins are always at a premium. They also provide an ideal method of distribution of stolen gold.

Despite Bank of England protests, Italy (and Switzerland until recently) holds that, as sovereigns are no longer legal tender in Britain, the making of counterfeit sovereigns is no offence as it cannot harm British currency. But in British Commonwealth countries the making of fake sovereigns is still an offence. The British authorities hold that, although the sovereign may not be legal tender within the United Kingdom, it is the best known coin in the world and accepted as good money anywhere. In Korea American airmen were issued with sovereigns in case they should land in enemy territory and need money to bribe their way back to freedom.

The official attitude in Italy is of immense value to the big gang of sovereign counterfeiters who fought and won their cases in the courts there. There is a vast quantity of stolen gold in any big community and if it can be given the easily negotiable form of a sovereign the major problem of selling it safely (and at *more* than the market price for the gold it contains) the crooks are in a position to make millions over a long period.

The greatest counterfeiting coup ever attempted was that organized by the Nazis, who planned to flood Europe and Britain with £200 million worth of £1, £5, £50 and £100 Bank of England notes. Some of these counterfeit notes are still being distributed in Europe, although police of all countries have co-operated in trying to stop their circulation. The German counterfeit plan was put into action in 1941, when Heinrich

Himmler, the Gestapo chief, ordered the printing of the notes to pay spies (among them was the agent known as Cicero, who was valet to the British Ambassador in Ankara) and to buy war materials from neutral countries. It was also planned to parachute them into Britain to disrupt the country's economy. But at the last moment the scheme went astray.

Official sources say that Britain was informed of the plot by intelligence agents, but the underworld believes it was a lucky chance that foiled the plan. Just as Hitler was ready to flood Europe with the fake notes, the British Treasury called in all large denominations to foil British black-marketeers. Whatever the reason, the counterfeit millions became almost worthless at that time.

The Nazis had collected three or four hundred of the world's most skilled forgers to do the job and made them work on the project in a "luxury" camp. When this centre of illicit skill was liberated by the Allies in 1945, the forgers drifted back to their own countries again or made their way to foreign capitals where they are working now.

The notes they made, with all the resources of the Gestapo and the Nazi regime to aid them in providing paper, presses and technical equipment, were excellent imitations. Huge numbers of the £5 notes are still circulating and only trained bank experts can pick them from legal fivers.

These are part of the stock which the Nazis failed to destroy when the war ended. The Nazis are said to have burned £180 million worth of the Gestapo notes, but £60 million is still a lot of counterfeit currency to be at large. Millions of the £5 notes were transhipped to Western Europe and the Americas at one stage from Poland, Egypt and China. The chief victims in this huge traffic, based on the foiled war-time currency coup, have been the European refugees who accepted the notes in good faith and took them out of their countries as easily portable assets when they set out in search of freedom.

German attempts to make counterfeit American dollar currency in the post-war years have failed largely because of the difficulty counterfeiters have in reproducing the paper on which dollar notes are printed. This paper includes minute coloured flecks, paper shreds of red, green and blue. Currency dealers of any experience can detect the spurious notes almost at a glance.

But the counterfeiters never stop trying. Dozens of hidden printing plants have been uncovered by police in France, Italy, Germany and Austria, and huge stacks of counterfeit dollars have been confiscated each year since 1945. Just as Poland has produced some of the most highly skilled pick-pockets in the underworld, and Greeks have won a reputation as the gambling professionals, so have Russians come to have a reputation as forgers. There is also, perhaps, some truth in the theory that the Corsican people have produced more forgers of top class than any other race. Some of the best twenty-dollar pieces in gold ever made outside the law were produced in the Warsaw ghetto during the war.

Two forgers have won themselves places in encyclopædias for their swindling exploits. One was the Frenchman, Alexandre Stavisky, who became a millionaire financier through his successes as a forger and swindler. His culminating venture was the floating of a 500 million franc bond issue in Bayonne to take over the city's municipal pawn shops and loan agencies. He would have succeeded, but a minor official suspected the authenticity of some of the documents and Stavisky retreated to this villa at Chamonix where he committed suicide in 1934. There were big political repercussions over this mammoth swindle and the French government fell, although Stavisky was not found guilty of fraud and forgery until two years after his death.

The other classic forger in recent European times was Ivar Kreuger, the Swedish match king who controlled 250 factories in 43 countries and amassed an enormous fortune. He financed loans on an international basis, lending 125 million francs to Germany, 75 million to France and 22 million to Yugoslavia, as well as smaller loans to other countries. After he killed himself in 1932 it was discovered that he had been forging documents and shares for years. His vast edifice of wealth was all an illusion. The incredible factor in these huge forging swindles is that officials, legal experts and the most astute diplomats were apparently as easy to fool as any average member of the public. This can be explained only by the fact that a good front and an appearance of wealth will lull almost any victims, or "marks" as they are called in the underworld, into a false sense of security.

The big swindlers are impressive, but the individual operators are more interesting. The recent case of the lone counterfeiter, Sydney Wainwright, the quiet, drab man of sixty-eight, who worked in the attic of his humble home in Leeds, is a good example of the odd personalities that lie behind ordinary outward appearances. Wainwright, who was jailed for fourteen years when he was convicted in 1955, made and distributed some of the finest forgeries of 10s. and £1 notes ever seen in England and he did it successfully for twenty-one years.

Shut away in his small terrace house, and hidden from his family in the little room he used as a workshop, were inks which he mixed himself, boxes of special paper, cameras, a small printing machine, a hand-press, a paraffin stove, a small mangle and the engraved plates he made so cleverly. Apart from his counterfeiting, it seems that Wainwright had no vices. He neither smoked nor drank, was very reserved and devoted his spare time to raising budgerigars and going for long walks alone.

A dull, uncommunicative man, the neighbours thought him. But when it came to his defence, his legal spokesman told the court that Wainwright was "an artist to his finger-tips", a man to whom forging notes was not so much a crime as a challenge to his skill. He could not bear to think that any task of draughtsmanship or engraving was beyond his powers. He had set out to make perfect 10s. notes in much the same way as a poet might aspire to compose a perfect sonnet.

Wainwright was fiercely proud of his art, and a strict perfectionist. He claimed that he destroyed far more notes than he uttered because they were not up to his best standard, although they could have been passed with little trouble. The notes he did pass were such good fakes that banks not only accepted them, but often issued them again as good currency.

Had an organized gang been able to use Wainwright he might have become a serious menace in England, but this silent, unassuming little man preferred to work alone, making and spending his fake money note by note as he needed the cash for household purchases. He is believed to have distributed thousands of them in the course of his secret years as a counterfeiter. Police and banks tracked down more than two thousand of his 10s. notes between 1934 and 1940, as well as nearly three hundred £1 notes.

Wainwright forgeries are still being discovered and he himself might still be making his money had not a sharp-witted shop-girl in a Leeds store noticed that a £1 note tendered for a block of chocolate had the prefix number M22E, one of the prefixes shops had been warned to look out for. It was Wainwright's wife who was arrested for offering the forged note and a search of the Wainwright home revealed the attic workship with all its incriminating evidence.

The judge said Wainwright was a vain and malicious man who took a delight in deceiving the Bank of England, but no-one can tell what strange motives drive a man like Wainwright to crime. It could not have been greed in his case as he could have made and issued far more spurious notes than he did. If he had been a normal criminal, he would have soon found a gang to exploit his talent on a business basis by buying materials and establishing a proper printing plant; and by organizing a team of expert note droppers all over Britain. Notes of the quality Wainwright made could have been sold in bulk all over Europe as, indeed, far less convincing forgeries have been.

But Wainwright liked the quiet, simple life of lonely walks, pet birds and drab surroundings. His great secret joy was in knowing that, in his own particular line, he was the best craftsman in England. This sort of man was as much out of touch with the underworld as he was with lawful society—a lonely eccentric whose gifts might have been used to a far greater extent in either community.

The lone forgers, working on a small scale and releasing only a few notes, may be eccentrics but there are a remarkably large number of them scattered throughout the world. Almost every community has them. While Wainwright was working Leeds, a strangely similar lone counterfeiter was operating in Sydney. This man, Charles Windeyer, made a series of £10 notes using the crudest of equipment, but great ingenuity and skill. He had a little technical training as a mechanic, but that was all. He picked up his knowledge of printings, photographic and etching processes in the public library over years of painstaking study and, by the same method, taught himself all he needed to know about inks and dyes and paper.

Like most counterfeiters he crumpled and soiled his fake notes well before he passed them. Although they were not good enough to stand more than a moment's scrutiny by a bank expert, they served well enough in the crush and bustle at race-tracks where, by using a £10 note for each £1 bet he laid, Windeyer was sure to win at least £9 on each race.

Windeyer did not have the intense pride in his craft that other lone forgers have, but he had a grudge against society generally for its refusal to accept him as a great inventor. His counterfeiting was largely prompted by a desire to prove that he was cleverer than people thought.

Vanity, revenge and greed are the main driving forces behind the counterfeiter who works alone, but the professional, the man who works as the skilled member of a criminal group, is a more straightforward personality in the eyes of other underworld crooks. As is the case in all branches of professional crime, the men and women involved in it never feel any compunction about robbing their victims because underworld standards are completely foreign to those of normal men and women.

One American counterfeiter, with more than thirty years of experience, confessed to a social worker once that there had been one occasion he regretted. This statement was so remarkable that the social worker, an earnest fellow absorbed in the psychology of the criminal mind, persuaded the crook to tell him what this incident was.

"I sold an old couple a parcel of forged bonds," the crook recalled. "They took me to the bank to draw out their money, nearly all their life's savings. And when we took a cab back to their home to settle up the deal the old lady jammed her fingers in the cab door as we got out at their front door. I've always felt sorry for the old dame. It must have been very painful, those jammed fingers."

"Crooks have as much human feeling for others as anyone else. Why should it seem strange that the forger felt sorry for the old woman's injury?" is what several professional crooks have commented when told that story. They, too, saw nothing deserving of pity in the old couple's financial plight. But they are often quick to defend the average crook for his kindness, sympathy and loyalty to other members of his racket.

Among pickpockets, for instance, it is unheard of to cut a man out of a share of the day's takings if he is prevented from playing his part because of illness. As long as the indisposed member of the gang was included in the arrangements to stage the day's thieving, the underworld code insists that he should be paid whether he plays his part or not. But any thought of the sufferings of the victims never enters their heads. This complete indifference to the feelings and rights of the public is as natural to the professional criminal as an honest man's indifference about the feelings of crooks locked up in gaol. The world looks different from the other side of the law.

An English counterfeiter, however, once astounded detectives by an odd spark of fair play. During the course of their investigations into this man's background, the police found in his home great stocks of uneaten breakfast food.

"Why have you got all this stuff?" one of the detectives asked the crook's wife.

"Siddy goes in for the competition," she said. "He's mad about winning a prize and you've got to have an end of a packet for every time you put in an entry."

The policeman was baffled. "Why doesn't he make his own packet-ends?" he asked. It would have been simple enough to forge, as far as the policeman could see, particularly for the man he was investigating whose forgeries were of the finest quality and included far more difficult imitations than the crude printing on a breakfast food packet.

"Oh, he'd never do that," said Siddy's wife, genuinely surprised at the policeman's suggestion. "It wouldn't be fair!"

Europe's counterfeiting plants are spread through half a dozen countries and many of them specialize in making American and South American currencies. In a recent Scotland Yard attempt to track down the makers of £5 notes, their inquiries led them to the south of France and then to a forger's den in Malta. And Buenos Aires contained, for many years, the best counterfeiter of Swiss francs in the world. This man, known to the trade by no other name than "David", sometimes sent his wife on a trip to Europe with a big supply of American Express travellers' cheques for distribution and sale in several capitals. David was originally a Belgian lithographer and learned his craft in Brussels.

Another forging group in South America specialized in copying American cheque forms and letters of credit with which they cleaned up a sizeable fortune a year or two ago. The crooks who deal in such forgeries operate as a highly efficient team and part of any such organization is always the "intelligence" branch. The men working in this department are probably the most thorough newspaper readers in the world. One of the elementary rules for good thieves, confidence men and crooks who peddle counterfeit currency and documents is, "always read the papers". A shrewd man picks up endless information about the movement of wealthy people, the development of financial deals and the movement of capital from one country to another. Ideas are always in demand in the underworld gangs, just as they are in legitimate businesses which depend on enterprise and enthusiasm for their survival and prosperity.

By knowing, a little in advance, what visitors are coming to a country (information which may be gleaned from social notes in the newspapers, inquiries at travel agencies and hotels) the smart counterfeiter can move in just ahead of the genuine traveller and, by impersonating him, clean up very profitably. Every time a big company issues new share capital you can be sure that there is a good chance that somewhere a counterfeiter is making bogus share certificates in the hope of unloading them, "at a special rate" to gullible investors anxious to get in on the ground floor.

The stream of stolen cheques which comes into receivers, and is passed on to forging experts, is often a valuable form of currency for the more highly expert gangs. The cheques are washed clean with special fluids, filled out afresh and newly signed. This form of robbery has become popular in all countries where people are anxious to acquire dollar credits in America and are prevented by currency restrictions from buying American dollars from their banks. Cheques on American banks are easy to sell to tourists and business men about to travel to America. Buying such cheques gives the purchaser a foolproof method of smuggling currency—or it would if the cheques were genuine. Cheques give the purchaser a most convenient access to dollar funds on his arrival in the United States—if it is a good cheque.

Forgeries of this sort need not be very skilful as the only people they need to convince are the purchasers, who have no way of checking on their authenticity. And when they find the cheque is worthless there is nothing they can do; to complain to the police would land them in trouble with the currency control authorities and to challenge the crooks themselves gets them nowhere. The stock answer is that the cheque was sold in good faith. "What you should have done, my dear sir, was sell it yourself as I did," is the usual bland reply.

British and other Sterling area countries have had to impose dollar restrictions of varying degrees since the war. Every time such a ban on the free exchange of currency is imposed the United States Treasury officials prepare for a new flood of forged notes.

The demand for black-market dollar bills of every denomination is always keen among migrants, refugees and tourists who can obtain only a limited supply of dollars through legitimate channels.

Many of the more expert forgers have travelled to Europe to work with Continental gangs, but even more have concentrated on producing fake dollars in the United States for export. The peak year for this huge trade in counterfeit was 1950, when more than two million counterfeit dollars were seized. They had been printed on more than two hundred different sets of plates and, although the fake money was seized largely in ports of entry to the United States, the tracking down of the plates and the crooks who distributed the counterfeit money has been by no means as easy.

Even though people carrying counterfeit can prove that they bought them in good faith and, perhaps, sacrificed all their assets for them, they are treated as smugglers. They are thus liable to far more severe penalties than for merely trying to break the currency restrictions. But this does not deter the "smart" businessman or tourist from buying dollars illegally; the risk of unknowingly buying counterfeit is a much greater risk than the risk of being caught carrying illegal dollar funds.

Berlin, when it was under the joint control of the Russians, Americans, British and French, was a paradise for the counterfeiters of Europe.

The city held, at one time, the cream of the forgery experts of the world. This situation produced a typical underworld reaction. Within a few months smugglers, counterfeiters and confidence men were operating, in a sort of loose combine, a monopoly in coffee, cigarettes and all foreign exchange and "hard" currencies.

The Berlin situation attracted some of the shrewdest operators in the world and their influence was considerable. They formed a kind of club, known to many as the Haus Brandenburg, and any professional crook who struck trouble would call on his friends to get him out of it. At one stage Haus Brandenburg did more business than the actual stock exchange. Its members telephoned European capitals and New York daily to check on the ruling official rates of exchange.

Police raided the club many times but rarely succeeded in holding any of their suspects. Lawyers defending the crooks were able to claim that their clients were the victims of Allied persecution and prejudice. Far from being smugglers or black-market operators in currency and counterfeit, they claimed, they were just unfortunate concentration camp victims trying to rehabilitate themselves in honest ventures.

The professional criminals who operate at the top level of international crime know how to exploit every legal defence of their schemes and it is seldom they who suffer the penalties of the law. The men behind the big counterfeit rings are never involved in the final distribution of fake notes to the public. They make their killings in the earlier stages by buying and selling the counterfeit stocks in bulk, paying perhaps 20 per cent of the notes, face value and selling them for about 50 per cent to the men who specialize in recruiting and organizing men and women to "drop" the counterfeit currency in cities all over the world.

One big gang was detected trying to flood Britain with forged 10s. and £1 notes in the spring of 1954. The first clue the police had of this coup was when a French girl was caught passing one of the forged notes in a West End shop and, on being searched, it was found she had a big roll of similar counterfeit money in her purse. She was one of a team of expert foreign women shoppers sent across as an advance party by the gang to test out the British reaction to the fake notes.

This woman's money was made by expert engravers and Scotland Yard experts suspected they might have come from some of the plates made during the war as part of Hitler's big plan to disorganize Britain's note circulation. Interpol officials claimed that the counterfeiters were a Maltese gang operating from Italy.

Advance "droppers" of notes are a regular feature of any big counterfeiting operation. They are paid on results, getting a percentage of the good money they bring back with them to the distributing agents. If anything goes wrong, a few women are punished for using fake notes but the ring remains untouched.

Until about a year ago one of the most successful women at this chancy business of passing forged notes was a beautiful Cuban who went under the single name of Rosita. She was an elegant woman with dark, flashing eyes and black hair. Any regular traveller on the shipping run between Buenos Aires and Cherbourg would have seen her about once every three months. She was always the most striking woman on board.

Rosita lived in a Buenos Aires apartment with two lovers, both Russians and both expert forgers of dollar bills. One went under the name of Sergei Vasilew and the other was known as The Jumping Jack because of his ability as a Cossack folk dancer.

The men were extremely skilled in uttering dollars up to the 20-dollar denomination and in forging travellers' cheques. As each new batch was completed in the apartment Rosita booked a passage on the next ship for Europe. Her job was twofold. First, she had to pass the forged dollars into the European market. Second, she had to pick up new supplies of the special paper the Russians used for the forgeries. The paper used in printing American dollars is, as explained earlier, very difficult to reproduce and that used by Rosita's companions was no exception. The forgeries were detectable at once in American banks. But the paper Rosita brought back from Europe was better than anything they could find in South America and as long as the forgeries were not passed to an expert the trio were safe.

Then one day something happened to upset their operations for all time. Rosita was away in Europe and the two Russians were working in their Buenos Aires apartment with the dwindling stocks of an earlier supply of paper. One of them had left the gas on in the kitchen . . .

Late that afternoon, police answering a neighbour's frantic call that there was a strong smell of gas in the block of flats, broke in and found the bodies of the two forgers slumped over their latest pile of phony dollars. Rosita never returned.

Apart from money, there is a big illegal trade in the forgery of works of art. This department of crime, like others which depend on an appearance of normal business, calls for crooks with personality and more than a smattering of culture. They must operate in highly expert circles and be able to retreat as nimbly as they advance should anything go wrong with their schemes.

It is difficult, in the world of art-dealers, to pick a professional crook from a man who is merely a sharp businessman; and it is even more difficult to prove in a court of law that a dealer who has been selling forgeries is a criminal. It is so easy for such a man to claim that he himself has been a victim of dishonest practice and is more to be pitied than accused of fraud. Because of this, and because many works of art have old and arguable origins, thousands of art forgeries remain undetected and are sold and re-sold through the years.

The tricking of art buyers in Paris has reached such proportions in recent years that the French Surété has created a special branch to deal with art criminals. At one of their recent public exhibitions, staged to impress on the public the danger of buying forged pictures, sculpture, rare books and fine china, and *objets d'art* generally, the police included forged coins, fake period furniture, bank notes, bonds, postage stamps and letters from famous people. The distorted talent represented in this collection was as great as the artistic merit in many a national gallery.

Here is one depaı tment of forgery which, for the forger, does not have the disadvantage that a man's skill must remain secret and unacknowledged by the experts and the art-loving public. Art, or rather, the commercial success of an artist, is an unpredictable thing. Capable craftsmen can starve as easily as they can prosper; individual success depends on the strange turns of artistic fashion. For an artist who fails to attract the attention of art-buyers, the imitation of successful work is little more than routine. It can become a profitable routine once the combination of a dishonest dealer is obtained.

The star exhibits in the display of frauds organized by the Paris police in 1955 were two counterfeit masterpieces by the Dutch art-forger Hans van Meegeren, the man who fooled the Nazi-leader Goering into paying nearly £1 million for a series of seven alleged Old Masters—three of them by Jan Vermeer—during the war. Van Meegeren might never have been revealed as a forger had it not been that Dutch authorities prosecuted him for selling national treasures to the Germans.

In his defence van Meegeren declared that the pictures in question were painted by himself, but, at first, the authorities would not believe him. Leading art experts could not agree among themselves whether the van Meegeren paintings were genuine or not and, at last, the forger was obliged to paint another "Vermeer" in his cell to prove his guilt as a forger. By doing this, van Meegeren was proving his innocence on the charges of collaboration—a unique twist in the history of justice by which the accused had to demonstrate guilt in the face of determined efforts by the prosecution to disbelieve him!

Van Meegeren's case has become a classic example of the forger's art for more reasons than the excellence of his skill. He was an artist who could not win recognition in his own right and he turned to forging pictures to spite the experts who refused to consider his own work seriously. To make his revenge complete, van Meegeren chose to forge paintings by the seventeenth century master, Vermeer, perhaps the most revered of all Dutch painters. Another reason van Meegeren picked on Vermeer to imitate was that no brushmarks are apparent in this Old Master's best work and van Meegeren knew his forgeries would have to pass all the modern tests of scrutiny such as the X-ray microscope, which can analyse the age of pigments and canvas.

Thus, van Meegeren wished to heal his wounded ego by tricking the greatest authorities and by tackling the most difficult subject to do so.

He bought seventeenth paintings of no particular merit to obtain the correct canvas for his forgeries and scrubbed them clean with pumice-stone and water, removing the paint without damaging the fabric.

He had to mix and grind his own pigments by hand to ensure that the microscope would reveal the particles as uneven, and not the regular, rounded shape characteristic of modern colour-making. His greatest problem was to attain the correct "ageing" of his painting. When completed the forged painting had to be impervious to the action of alcohol, it had to contain cracks and the hard gloss of two centuries of age. Van Meegeren tried hundreds of substances to achieve these effects and finally settled on resin as the element he needed. Then came six months of experimental baking in ovens to discover at which temperature the paint would crack and harden without discolouring the paint.

Van Meegeren's first "Vermeer" was begun in 1937 and the subject was *The Disciples at Emmaus*. He collected only seventeenth century objects to include in the picture and chose as his models a series of poor, illiterate people who would not know what was going on and would thus not be likely to betray his scheme.

The "Vermeer" was painted in seven months and (here again the procedure is a textbook example of the underworld's smooth approach to fraud) sent to a bank in Paris. A well-established lawyer was asked to handle the transaction with the greatest discretion. The painting, it was said, belonged to an old but fanatically proud French family who did not wish it known they were forced to sell their inherited art treasures. The painting passed all tests and Boyman's Museum in Amsterdam paid £68,000 for it. To explain his sudden wealth, van Meegeren told friends he had won a lottery and, later, when more of his forgeries were sold, he used the same excuse.

His original intention was realized—he had fooled the experts. But now greed dominated his life and he decided not to tell the story of the fakes after all. Three years after he sold his first forgery, van Meegeren was paid £116,000 by a millionaire art collector for *The Last Supper*.

From then on van Meegeren stepped up his rate of production, painting almost carelessly and inventing an entirely new period for Vermeer. All this in the land of Vermeer and under the learned noses of some of the most respected art connoisseurs in Europe! Tricking the Nazi art-looters was easy for such a consummate counterfeiter.

At his trial, van Meegeren complained to the police that other forgers were making more van Meegeren fakes as a market for the famous forgeries quickly developed. As usual, the underworld had lost no time in seizing a new opportunity for profit.

Van Meegeren was sentenced to one year's gaol and died before he was released. Within a few years, another great art scandal rocked Europe when a forger called Lother Maoskat, and three art experts, were charged with forging thirteenth century frescoes on a church wall in Lubeck, Germany.

These frauds have elements of genuine artistic passion which, it may be suggested, remove them from the scope of underworld cunning, but they throw an important light on the underworld. They demonstrate perfectly how crooks find it possible to exploit even the highest fields of human endeavour.

The art business operates largely on the basis of trust in an expert's opinion. The public does not pretend to know genuine art from the forged variety and any crook who is capable of posing as an art dealer has hundreds of wealthy victims at his mercy. The forgeries do not need to be of Old Masters to be profitable. Any modern painter whose pictures are selling well will do as a model for the forgers and the field is wide open at all times for trickery.

The people engaged in this form of counterfeiting are, of all the underworld types, nearest to the average man and woman in their outlook. They operate on the fringe of both worlds—the honest and the criminal. Art forgers are of no value to the average crook and they have no need of any contacts with other branches of the criminal community. They seldom strike trouble with the police because their victims seldom realize they have been robbed until long after the sale has taken place. Even then, they are reluctant to advertise their stupidity. In most cases the victims keep quiet and often try a little double-dealing themselves in order to cut their losses.

Wealthy tourists visiting Paris, Brussels, Berlin and other art-dealing centres are always fair game for the culture counterfeiters. South American diplomats, many of whom like to build up assets in the form of valuable paintings and other works of art, are ideal victims. Big collectors almost inevitably buy a lot of worthless junk, as well as genuine art treasures, as they are in the hands of dealers who earn a commission on everything purchased.

The men who carry out the deals in forged paintings are much more of the underworld than the painters they commission to do the bogus work. The art world is an ideal haven for the confidence man. He is operating among other confidence men, but the crook is a professional and the art experts and dealers are mere amateurs. They are, in many ways, easier to exploit than the man who does not pretend to know anything about art, except, of course "what he likes".

The only safe rule for the man who wishes to buy genuinely valuable paintings is the rule that wise diamond buyers follow: Never make a purchase without the advice of an expert you can trust.

11

thieves and receivers

WE have considered the main specialists of crime in the underworld. Now we must turn our attention to the rank and file of the criminal society which surrounds the lives of all of us—the ordinary burglars and thieves. This vast group, by far the most numerous class in the underworld, also happens to be the least skilled. There are exceptions, as we shall see, but, speaking generally, straight out theft, uncomplicated by the various ruses and techniques necessary to other types of crooks, demands nothing but persistence and enough brains to seize an opportunity when it occurs.

Confidence men must be able to act; safe-breakers need technical knowledge and equipment; cardsharpers must have manual dexterity and wonderful nerve; smugglers need organizations and good appearance; pickpockets need daring and a delicate touch; forgers need artistic ability. But the common thief, and there are millions of them in the world to-day, needs nothing but the basic underworld belief that the risk of prison is better than the drudgery of work.

Thieves (we use the term in its widest sense to include any type of theft from train robbery to hi-jacking, from sneak-thieving to raids on wealthy homes and warehouses) are nearly always unkempt, rough looking men. They do not need to make a good impression on anyone in their business. They are the labourers of the underworld.

Almost their only concern is to remain unknown to the police and, for this reason, professional thieves will take any amount of trouble not to show their faces to their victims. It is the amateurs who pose as telephone mechanics, gas-meter readers or plumbers to gain entry to a dwelling and size up its possibilities.

Professional thieves mix with all members of the underworld from time to time, but their main contact is with the receivers, a class of crook we shall discuss more fully later in this chapter. Most burglars are local people and thieving is one branch of the underworld where women play no part in the day to day operations which, taken together, make up the bulk of modern crime. Estimates are obviously bound to be little more than guesswork, but it is interesting to notice that officials claim that professional thieves take a haul of about £13 million a year in and around London and £35 million a year in New York, to name only the two biggest cities of the world. These estimates are based on the totals of crime known to the police; there are many more thefts of one sort and another that are never reported.

Another characteristic peculiar to the habitual burglar is that he seldom moves away from his own city and hardly ever out of his own country. Such enterprise would demand a degree of ability and initiative that the average thief knows nothing about. Psychological tests among thieves in prison shows that their average intelligence quotient is between 70 and 90 (100 is the score for the average intelligent man or woman) and, as one doctor put it, "they are not considered clever except by themselves".

This is true of the attitude toward burglars and common thieves held by the underworld's specialists. Thieves are considered easy game for the gamblers, pickpockets and receivers. The larger share of stolen property goes into the hands of other crooks within a few days of the thief's robbery. The thieves who do exceed these average levels of skill and intelligence always develop other attributes in the criminal world; they either acquire the presence and appearance of confidence men or become expert technicians in some branch of the underworld's trades.

The mass of thieves are a shiftless, improvident lot, but they have an even, cheerful temperament. If a burlgar loses his money at the gaming table, or is cheated out of his loot, he merely shrugs and plots another raid. If he is caught and jailed he accepts his fate with resignation and spends most of his time in prison planning new robberies for the time when he is released.

The efficient thief, of course, achieves a considerable measure of skill in picking locks and forcing entry silently. He also becomes very shrewd about avoiding, or dismantling, alarm systems. These departments of knowledge are as much part of his equipment as jemmies and soft-soled shoes and, although his skills are relatively elementary compared to the art and precision of the professionals in other types of criminal activity, it is surprising how well they work.

Lock-picking is not difficult to learn and there are plenty of tutors in the underworld. Even patent locks, for which only one pattern of key will do, may be opened by a very simple expedient which involves no more elaborate piece of equipment than a strip of tough celluloid. This, in the hand of a practised man, can be inserted between the door jamb and the lock to push the "tongue" of the lock back and thus open the door.

Experienced burglars may not need any great degree of skill to gain entry to premises, but they do devote a great deal of time to studying the layout of a job and to discovering as much as they can about their proposed victims. Here again, the methods are simple. They watch patiently to discover how many people live in a house or flat, and telephone to check whether there is anyone at home before they call.

Some idea of the basic skills a burglar needs was revealed in New York a few years ago when a so-called "professor of burglary"—an ex-convict known as Louis Mainiari—was found to be running a school for thieves. His printed curriculum included lessons in how to choose and "case" a job, how to break in safely, how to force desks, cash boxes and small safes, and how to make a quick getaway. There is less formality about the lessons the veterans give the beginners in other cities, but it is normal practice in the underworld for youths to be taken under the wing of experienced burglars and taught the tricks of the trade.

This trend became particularly noticeable in London following the passing of the Criminal Justice Act after the war—a piece of legislation designed to weed out the veterans by imposing longer sentences on them. What happened was that old lags suddenly disappeared from the every-day scene of robbery and younger men and youths took their place, acting under instruction from the "masters". As usual, none of the arrested culprits would talk; loyalty to the underworld code develops early in a criminal's career.

A typical burglar, known to the underworld as Harry the

Climber, explained his attitude in these words: "I done a few jobs when I was a youngster and got caught a few times. So I got a record. It's no use me trying to go straight now, never has been since I become known. I've only got to be seen walking past some of the boys and the coppers grab me for consorting. Or they'll come and pick on me whenever someone's done a job, just in case it's me.

"What we reckon is that if you're going to be in trouble all the time with the cops, you may as well do something to be in trouble *for*. Sometimes you do a job and get away with it, sometimes you don't. But if you're not doing anything you get all the trouble and none of the breaks. It stands to reason you've got to pull a few jobs to get anywhere".

In twenty years of burglary, Harry the Climber has spent nine years in gaol. "But I never been mug enough to work for a living," he said.

Harry was one of the run-of-the-mill thieves, robbing small shops and modest homes and, occasionally, a warehouse for cigarettes or liquor. But only in small quantities as he operated alone. The gangs demand a higher standard of performance than Harry could provide and groups of thieves have a better record of success.

One Paris gang had quite a team of tradesmen to call on—locksmiths, carpenters and electricians. They specialized in raiding flats of well-to-do people and their intelligence system was thorough. They watched the papers to note when society people went on holiday, they had inside contacts among servants and cleaners and, if there was a safe to be cracked they would call in a safe-breaker and pay him a special cut of the takings. They would not tackle a job with any great element of risk, and, unless they knew a place was vacant and the getaway assured, they would refuse to act. They worked together for years until an informer ended their most profitable business.

Other groups make a speciality of raiding warehouses, big shops and fur stores. These groups generally comprise four or five men and they concentrate on taking goods that have a quick re-sale value. They work mainly with the aid of information from within the firms they rob, for, as they plan their operations to include the handling of large quantities of furs, or liquor, materials or tobacco, they cannot afford to mistime their raids. They never go "blind" into a job. They know almost to the minute how much uninterrupted time they have to force an entry, seize their haul and load it into waiting vehicles. It is amazing how many furs or how many bolts of material can be lifted in fifteen minutes when an operation is well organized.

There are some Continental partnerships which do operate on "spec", but they rob only homes in wealthy areas and steal only jewellery or furs in a series of lightning raids. All they make sure of is that they have a clear quarter of an hour or twenty minutes to make their raid and get away. A Spaniard, who now lives in South America and is known as El Tigre, was an outstanding "blind" raider who was lucky enough to stumble on three or four rich hauls of jewellery and amass enough money to leave France and set up in a gambling business in Sao Paulo.

Another burglar, known well in Rome's underworld as Istanbul Jack, made a reputation for himself because of his fabulous memory for places and an uncanny sense of direction. He was an illiterate and a somewhat dull-witted fellow, but he worked with a gang and brought off some remarkable robberies. The system was that, during the day, the gang would drive past a likely residence in a locality where Istanbul Jack had never been. A place would be pointed out to him and the group would then drive back to their headquarters in a poor area of the city. That night Istanbul Jack would set out alone and, unaided by any guiding, would find his way to the job without a moment's hesitation.

In this way the gang avoided the greatest of all dangers that beset burglary—the risk of being noticed while looking the proposed job over to work out a means of entry and an easy getaway route. He worked in this way for some time until he realized that he was taking all the risks and getting only a small share of the proceeds. He was cunning enough, eventually, to do a job and then keep all the loot for himself. But he was no match for the gang and he was killed in a brawl a few days after his attempt to double-cross them.

Professional burglars, outside of America, generally go un-armed and avoid violence of any sort whenever possible. If a watchman has to be put out of action, the man assigned to the job does it as gently as he can and makes sure the victim receives no serious injury. The big increase in warehouse and dockside robberies that developed all over the world after the war were not organized by professional thieves alone; the brains behind all big raids were nearly always black-market operators—criminals of a superior underworld class who lured the raiders into such projects with promises of big rewards. The planning of a robbery of any size takes far more leadership and executive ability than the average burglar possesses. The problem of how to realize on the stolen property is also too great a hurdle for the typical thief whose contacts with receivers, or "fences", is limited to men who accept and handle only small quantities of booty at a time. We shall see, in due course, how the big receivers unload stolen goods in large lots.

A distinctive, though small class of burglars, is made up of the sneak-thieves. This is a strange group whose best performers often achieve big reputations among their fellow crooks for coolness and daring. The sneak-thief is generally a small and, oddly enough, nervous man when he is not on a job. But he works to a system which makes most other criminals feel uneasy just to contemplate the risks it involves.

Sneak-thieves slip into a house, generally in the late afternoon or early evening, and stay concealed for several hours before they move into action. Sometimes they wait until the household is asleep and then, moving with expert caution, they rifle clothes, drawers and wallets within a few feet of their unconscious owners. At other times, they wait merely until the family is gathered in one room—round a fire or watching television or listening to the wireless—and proceed to strip bedrooms of anything valuable.

The basic skill these thieves must have is the ability to move without making a sound and this, in itself, has become a specialized branch of knowledge. Deliberate, balanced movement and a delicate sense of touch are essential to a man who is opening doors and walking about on floors only a few feet away from a group of people, any one of whom might suddenly decide to leave the room they are in and come to the section of the house where the sneak-thief is working. Such men have an acute ear for the slightest alteration in the noise pattern of a conversation, the tone of a wireless heard through a closed door or the breathing of a domestic pet. They must also have fine sense of direction as, in an emergency, they may have to move swiftly and silently in the dark to hide or escape.

One of the London underworld's favourite stories of a sneak-thief is that which concerns a wealthy and elderly bookmaker who lived in rooms in a hotel just off Piccadilly. Someone, it seems, had tipped the thief off about the bookie's habit of carrying a big sum of money in notes of large denomination in his hip-pocket and of his custom of hanging his trousers over a chair near his bed without bothering to remove the money when he went to sleep. The sneak-thief, a young Irish boy widely known for his daring, managed to secrete himself under the bookmaker's bed during the afternoon and lay there until his victim arrived late at night.

He waited until he was sure the old man was asleep and then inched his way out into the middle of the room without making a sound. He found the trousers, as he had been advised, over the back of a chair. Although he had to ease the roll of money out at a distance of only a few inches from the sleeping man's nose, he managed it neatly. The Irish lad was working his way backwards across the room to the door when the bookmaker sat up in bed, switched on the light and bounded out of the bedclothes to grab the youth by the scruff of the neck.

The bookmaker towered over the thief in a great rage and demanded his money back. He got it without a murmur from the thief, who expected he would be handed over to the police. But the bookmaker, who knew a lot about the underworld, was not primarily concerned with the Irish lad—he wanted to know who it was who had told him how to go about his theft. The boy would not tell him, but the bookmaker finally let him go and, as he was about to leave, handed him £50 as "insurance" against another attempt.

It was money well spent. The Irish boy did not fail to appreciate the old man's generosity and repaid it by not saying a word about his experience until the bookmaker died a year or so later. "If I'd told anyone how easy he was to rob there'd have been a queue to get into his room," he said. "And the top-off (informer) who sent me there would have put someone else on the old chap if he'd known I failed to get his roll. He wanted the old boy to be robbed merely because he disliked him."

The lone operators in burglary are not as numerous as it would appear. Many a thief likes to boast that he carried out a job unaided when, in fact, he was merely one of a group and, probably, a subordinate one at that. But there are individualists in the burglary racket and one of them who deserved his reputation as a man of considerable courage was the Riviera jewel thief and cat-burglar, Mario Sambucco. He was a suave and agile crook who was finally arrested with his jemmy and lock-picking gear snugly tucked under his white dinner jacket in a big hotel.

Sambucco claimed he spent two hours a day climbing trees to keep himself in good condition for his drainpipe and window-ledge excursions into the rooms and flats of wealthy tourists and stage stars. He mixed in fashionable circles, or hovered on the fringes of them, to gather his information. French police admitted that Sambucco had stolen £100,000 worth of jewellery before he was caught, and jailed for eight years, in 1953.

Perhaps the most successful organizer of jewel thefts in Britain in recent years was Bertie Holliday (also known as Barry Fieldsend) whose gang carried out one of the biggest jewel robberies of the twentieth century, just after World War II. His victims included members of the nobility.

After Holliday committed suicide, while out on bail, Scotland Yard arranged an exhibition of part of his loot, valued at £50,000, so that owners could claim their property. This remarkable collection was only one man's share of a series of big gem thefts which totalled £467,000 in the year 1949 alone.

Before we discuss the huge operations of the receivers, it might be as well to refer to the huge thieving industry conducted by hi-jackers, the men who rob lorries as they travel the highways. This form of crime reaches staggering proportions in America where millions of pounds worth of goods are stolen in this way. The United States transport a big proportion of goods by road and one example of how the hi-jackers work will demonstrate the efficiency of their methods.

A large van, carrying £50,000 worth of silk material, pulled up when the lights were against it at a cross-roads outside Chicago. A big limousine drew up alongside the lorry and two armed men leaped into the cabin of the lorry, ordering the driver and his mate to get out. They shoved the two men into the car and then drove the lorry away themselves, leaving the driver and his assistant in the car. They were later found bound and beaten at the side of a lonely road and the load of silk was never traced. The whole operation of seizing the lorry took only half a minute, the time the lights stayed red at the intersection.

Men who can carry out such split-second operations are fortunately rare, but other highway robberies occur every day and without violence. Trucks and lorries are seized and driven away while the drivers are out of their cabins for only a few moments by men who study the habits of transport workers in great detail, watching loading points and rest places for weeks to find a weakness in the system. A few seconds in which a vehicle is left unattended is all the opportunity they need. These thefts, and raids on warehouses and shops, jumped from £3 million in Britain in 1939 to £13 million in 1949—an indication of the effect of war on organized crime.

A similar upsurge in thefts has been recorded in many other countries, but the reason is not entirely that ex-soldiers have taken to crime. War unsettles civilians as much as it unsettles servicemen, and recruits to the underworld are gathered in from both classes of citizens in times of international upheaval.

The constant flow of stolen goods is enormous and the business of receiving them has developed into a major business. Whether the loot is a handful of precious stones or several bales of material, crates of whisky or cartons of cigarettes, the receivers know where to hide it and where to sell it. Receivers are a necessary evil to the thieves and sometimes finance their big ventures for them. But the receiver is not a popular character among criminals. He always drives a ruthlessly hard bargain and there is no other way for the crook to realize on his booty. The receiver claims with some justification, that he takes enormous risks in handling stolen goods and that he deserves every penny he makes.

They have to be specialists. Some will deal in nothing but furs, others stick to jewels and yet others have extensive markets in material, tobacco and liquor and precious metals. Some are receivers for receivers—accepting anything the crooks bring in and channelling it to the men who specialize in various goods on the underworld's huge network of markets. There are receiver's agents who do nothing but hide goods for a set fee, accepting a sealed parcel and agreeing to hold it for £10 or £20 a week until it is picked up. They do not know what the package contains, they do not know the men who leave it or the men who pick it up; and they do not want to know these things. Bulkier goods are often hidden in most ingenious places in the country. One agent kept a pig-sty full of silks and stolen gowns, another had a haystack full of liquor and cigarettes.

There are many buyers for stolen property. Shopkeepers in times of shortages are always a good market for cigarettes and food. Clothing makers can very often be interested in bulk supplies that are delivered discreetly, free of sales tax. Apart from these markets, the big receivers can find other buyers. They can hold stocks of jewellery and furs for long periods until it is safe to distribute them locally or overseas.

The receivers of furs do not always deal with thieves direct, but collect the stolen goods from intermediaries on the principle that the less the crooks know about receivers' big stocks of furs, the better. It is not unusual for a gang of burglars to raid a receiver's hidden warehouse.

When stolen fur coats are gathered in, the receiver passes them over to crooked furriers who re-model the coats to sell them to the public. Men dealing in this line of business are, naturally, expert furriers and they know their markets as well as any legitimate dealer. Seeing that they pay about one-tenth of the value for the furs and sell them at about 80 per cent of their value they are on a good thing.

Receivers of diamonds are another class of specialists who will not bother to trade in any other type of jewellery, apart, in some instances, from pearls. The diamond receivers dismantle the gold and platinum settings regardless of their value as works of art and melt these precious metals down into bars for sale to the gold and platinum buyers. If the diamonds are large, and therefore easier to trace and identify, they are often re-cut and re-set for sale to the jewellery tiade through some apparently reputable dealer. Bracelets and necklaces are nearly always re-made and some of the work done by receivers' craftsmen is as fine as any done elsewhere.

The price paid for stolen gems is about one-tenth of their value and, although the victims generally inflate the value of their losses (to boost their insurance claims) the thief has little chance of impressing his underworld friend, the receiver, with such statements. If a newspaper report records the value of jewels stolen at £10,000 the burglar will be lucky to get £1,000 for his haul—and he dare not argue too violently with the receiver.

Both parties to such deals regard each other as highly untrustworthy, but it is the receiver who has the whip hand. He is generally a man of some substance with a good "front". He has far more chance of having his word taken as an informer than the uncouth, and probably already suspect, burglar. If a burglar threatens to make trouble for the receiver he not only fails to sell his loot to him, but often finds that other receivers have been warned off him as well. And when he stages his next job, he may find the police are waiting for him because he has been under observation. Receivers are hard men, working in a hard trade and they have no mercy if they think a customer has gone away disgruntled and, perhaps, thinking of revenge.

Other classes of stolen valuables, such as watches, cigarette cases and silver and gold plate all get different treatment. Watches may have their maker's numbers filed out before they are re-sold, or the movements may be thrown away and the gold cases smelted down. Gold cigarette cases and gold plate are always smelted down into bars. Receivers deal with all types in the underworld and the variety of goods they are asked to buy would be bewildering if one man tried to deal in every field of stolen property. Pickpockets bring in personal jewellery, travellers' cheques; burglars bring in every type of article from bonds to bracelets and pearls to paintings; safe-breakers demand cash for the "hot" money they deliver, accepting big discounts in cases where the stolen notes are new and are likely to have their numbering recorded. (In such cases the receiver must be prepared to hold the stolen money for long periods and release it little by little; for doing this he expects to clear at least 300 per cent on the deal and safe-breakers and bank-robbers sometimes get even less than 25 per cent of the face value of the money they steal.)

Shoplifting gangs and hi-jackers bring in a flow of bulk goods—materials and luxury items—which demand careful and highly expert handling. The receiver dealing in these commodities has dozens of contacts—varying from his underworld agents who contact the thieves, to his entirely respectable business clients who buy the stolen articles on good faith, just as they would from a legitimate wholesaler. In some cases the receiver sells cheap to other agents in this trade, the degree of risk diminishing as the goods change hands each time on their way back to the normal trading world. In most cases the run-over is swift, as the sooner stolen goods are split up and unloaded the better. But some receivers must carry part of their stocks for a long time before they can dare to move them. For this prolonged risk they demand big rewards.

It might seem that raw materials are harder to dispose of than finished goods, but this is seldom the case. A recent example of the fate of a number of bales of wool, loaded at an Australian port, demonstrates how a shrewd receiver can handle business with little delay if he knows his business. In this case the receiver already had a customer—a Hungarian cloth manufacturer—before he sent out the word that he would be interested in buying stolen bales. A waterfront gang of thieves went into operation almost immediately. By bribing a tally clerk they managed to divert several lorry-loads of baled wool as they were about to be loaded into a ship bound for England.

The lorry-drivers got their delivery receipts from the clerk and then drove the wool to a special corner of the storage shed. From there it was picked up by the thieves, working in broad daylight and unnoticed among the bustle of the dockside work, and taken to the receiver. He had it delivered to his Hungarian buyer, who made his own arrangements to have the wool woven into material. The theft was discovered soon after the ship arrived in London and police conducted an extensive check at every port of call on the journey, thinking the wool had been stolen in Colombo or the Middle East. But by the time they began their inquiries the stolen wool had been woven, made into clothing and was on sale in retail shops in half a dozen Australian cities.

To the thieves, the stolen wool would have been useless and they would never have considered taking it unless the receiver had asked them for it. But with his business contacts, the theft became a highly profitable one. Without receivers, nearly all classes of thieves would be helpless and it is no wonder that the legal penalties for receiving stolen property are so severe in all countries. The police know what a vital part they play in the economy of the underworld and, although the risk is great for such crooks, they can count on a considerable degree of protection.

They know they are disliked by most criminals, but they also know they are indispensable. Being, in the main, far more astute and knowledgeable in the field of distribution and sale, receivers know burglars and thieves will accept what they are offered and will seldom complain. The thief's casual acceptance of the risks of his trade and his carefree belief that "there is always something to steal" if he runs short of funds, keeps the receivers busy even in the worst of times.

Fences make enormous profits on everything they handle, but although they claim they run big risks they know that they have a better than even chance of success. Underworld experience varies according to the individual's cunning and skill, but it is generally accepted that 60 per cent of crime goes undetected. Of the 40 per cent that *is* detected, quite a proportion goes unpunished for lack of evidence in the courts.

Experienced criminals claim that of the 40 per cent of detected crime, 30 per cent is reported by informers and only 10 per cent is discovered by the police. These estimates have been confirmed by legal authorities on crime and many of them claim that the modern police methods of squad cars and extensive telephone contacts and radio patrols are not as valuable in the war against the underworld as the old system of paying "coppers' narks" for their information and having plenty of men on the beat. The much maligned local policeman is far more likely to develop contacts with informers than the flying squad experts and, if the local policeman were given authority to pay for his information where necessary, the percentage of detected crime might well rise.

The fact that more than half the crime committed in civilized countries goes undetected is not so much a reflection on the efficiency of the police systems as it is on the general moral standards of the community at large. F.B.I. chief, J. Edgar Hoover, has admitted that America has six million known crooks—one in twenty-three of the population of the United

States! This great ocean of criminal enterprise can hardly be kept in serious check by a few thousand policemen.

The greatest proportion of any nation's underworld is made up of the ordinary thief or burglar, whose greatest weakness, as we have noted, is his lack of brains. Police often issue incorrect information to the newspapers when they are searching for a criminal in the hope that the underworld will believe what it reads, the way most honest citizens do. By stating that they are looking for a certain man in connection with a crime, the police sometimes lull the real culprit into a sense of false security. They name a man whom they know is innocent and wait to see if the real suspect becomes careless. He often does and, coming out of hiding in the happy belief that he is not wanted for a particular job, he is apprehended. Such simple ruses work remarkably frequently with the ordinary thief, but the specialists in crime do not fall for these tricks. They are always wary and, through their wide contacts in the underworld, generally closely and well informed. But, although the average thief may not be very bright, he abounds in such numbers that the bulk of ordinary crime is committed by his kind.

Receivers mix with both the underworld and the normal world, often appearing in polite society as self-made men. They may seem a little rough to really respectable people, but they are accepted in most circles. It is hard to believe that a man of means can be a crook, at least it is hard to believe of a man who courts the attention of other wealthy people and makes no attempt to live his life away from the public gaze. But it is in such company and in such a manner that the really successful receivers glean much of their information and make most of their business contacts.

These key-men in the underworld spend as much of their time in polite society and the normal commercial world as they do in the underworld and, being used to dealing with the criminal personalities, they are well able to cope with even their shrewdest legitimate business acquaintances. Some of the most successful thieves and burglars have owed their success to a blending of legitimate information and illegal enterprise. A partnership in which one man contributes knowledge and the other contributes criminal daring is the toughest combination the police can meet.

An outstanding example of this fruitful blending of talents was the case of a man known to the underworld in Britain as *Peter the Plotter* and, to the authorities, as Harold Lough White. White, now in prison for his part in a £37,000 robbery of platinum and gold leaf from a London firm, was a doctor's son. At the height of his success as a burglar, he lived an expensive life and a very social one. His big chance came when he met up with an insurance broker who had a book that most burglars know nothing about and those who do only dream about getting a chance of reading. The broker's book was an insurance survey, published for private circulation among Lloyd's insurance underwriters. It listed detailed particulars of insured valuables. And next to each entry were details of burglar alarm systems, security patrols, telephones and the routines of cashiers in locking safes and strong-rooms.

The book contained everything an insurance broker needed to know to calculate the risk of theft in each case. The combination of White's criminal enterprise and the knowledge in the book founded a partnership that robbed country houses, shops and factories with uncanny success for months. White and his broker friend enlisted the aid of two professional cracksmen whose tools of trade included oxy-electric steel cutters, transformers to boost voltages wherever the steel cutters were plugged in, a special lighted probe for exploring locks, welding gear, gloves, aprons and an assortment of cables, fuses, plugs and drills to adapt the heavier equipment to any setting.

The gang worked so efficiently that police suspected each job was carried out with the aid of inside information and it was only by especially clever detection that the gang was finally brought to book. It began by a policeman noting the number of White's sleek car late one night in Savile Row and connecting this with the fact that the firm robbed of the platinum and gold, a jewel factory, was in the same street. A police check on White's flat and his country cottage revealed the valuable insurance register and the broker's telephone number.

At the broker's home police found copied extracts from the register and an informer led them to one of the safe-breakers. This crook was trapped because dust from the drilled safe was traced in the grease of his hair-comb, and the fourth member of the gang, the other cracksman, had the same type of dust in the turn-ups of his trousers.

This was burglary of unique distinction, detected by a combination of classic police methods—observation of the man on the beat, science and the ubiquitous informer. But the underworld was not entirely defeated in this affair—when the police were led to White's hiding place for the loot, a clump of shrubs in the garden of his country cottage in Buckinghamshire, they found only the settings of the stolen rings. The diamonds had all been removed.

Although professional housebreakers and thieves are not given to violence they have a weapon of revenge which is particularly vicious—this is the spiteful wrecking of an enemy's home and possessions.

Surprised on a job, the expert thief thinks only of escape. Only by running away can he hope to preserve his anonymity and it is this quality which gives him, perhaps, half his power. Once identified, a burglar loses, as it were, the most valuable item of his stock-in-trade. As long as he is not known to the police he is free to move about in almost any locality and able to size up prospective jobs without fear of rousing suspicion. Seeing that professionals always study the outside of premises very carefully before they go into action, this ability to observe the buildings is most valuable to them. An experienced man can work out the best means of entry and exit (including emergency exits in case of interruption on the job) in the smallest detail, calculating the numbers of steps he will need to take from window to door and from room to room long before he sets foot in the house. This knowledge, which he acquires by painstaking study and deliberation before tackling a job of any size, stands him in good stead when he starts work in the dark. It accounts, in many instances, for the remarkably quick getaways burglars stage when being chased.

To stay and show fight when disturbed would be fatal to the burglar, for then he would almost certainly give his victim a glimpse of his face. The thugs who do assault their victims receive little respect in the underworld as craftsmen in their trade. But this perpetual need for flight, rather than aggression, seems to develop a malicious desire to injure enemies by assaulting their property rather than their person. Prosecuting counsel, magistrates and judges are always possible targets for the vengeful burglar; so, on occasions, are the receivers who have cheated him too ruthlessly.

There is hardly any more effective way of wounding a sensitive and intelligent man (short of serious injury) than to ruin his most treasured possessions. Book, pictures, documents, clothing, collections of one sort and another, all suffer when a home is wrecked as an act of revenge. The damage can reach untold proportions in a few minutes. Curtains are ripped, china smashed, clothing tipped in a heap and stained with ink and other fluids, taps left running to swamp carpets and ruin ceilings, windows and mirrors are broken and walls smeared with tar and paint. Gramophones, radios and television sets and other items of expensive equipment are hammered into useless junk by some of these men expressing their violent hatreds in wanton destruction.

The total money cost of damage in such cases runs into thousands of pounds—a far more effective way of inflicting a loss on an enemy than by stealing his possessions. Stealing involves the risk of being caught with the goods, but wrecking is not only psychologically satisfying for a depraved mind, but also safe. A man who has destroyed the contents of a home walks away from it bearing not a sign of his guilt and, as they generally choose victims who have probably dozens of underworld grudges held against them, the suspect can reasonably expect to escape detection in the safety of numbers. Destruction of valued objects is one of the most primitive urges of man and, to experts in the criminal personality, the sort of expression of hatred most likely to be found among the underworld's simplest citizens, the burglars.

One other type of thieving deserves special mention in these days of modern transport—car thefts. In Britain, America and other countries where the average man is a car owner, every automobile represents an easily available concentration of wealth. Diamond necklaces, bankrolls and fur coats are not left parked along the highways and byways of every town and city, a constant temptation to crooks. But motor-cars, in the hands of the men who specialize in this form of theft, are just as easily negotiable as these other valuable possessions and they are always available.

Car thieves are often members of gangs who need transport for other crime, and such crooks never move about except in stolen cars. If they are wrecked, the gang loses nothing, and to travel in an honest citizen's car is a useful form of protection. They can open any car and do not need ignition keys. It is as easy as taking fruit off the sideboard for the professional to have a powerful car always at his command, and the veterans at the game take a car as frequently and calmly as normal people take a taxi. In some jobs, the gang drives to a central point in one lot of stolen vehicles and picks up a new lot for its raid and getaway. This helps confuse the police, who often set out to look for the first batch of cars while the crooks are escaping in a second lot.

The car thieves who merely drive automobiles and then abandon them are one part of the car robbery group; the men who steal cars and proceed to dismantle them, disguise them and resell the parts or the complete vehicle are another branch of the trade. These men are skilled mechanics and generally work in quite large groups comprised of thieves, mechanics and salesmen. Within twenty-four hours a car in good condition can be altered and sold to legitimate car dealers in second-hand vehicles, its registration papers forged and the "owners" credentials improvized. There are two victims in such operations: the original owner and the innocent purchaser who finds, if the car is traced, that he has invested his money in property to which he has no legal title. The washing of car registration documents and the forging of new details of engine number, make and other descriptive items is a profitable sideline for the experts in counterfeit documents. These men are always available to car theft groups through the normal contact links any professional criminal acquires as soon as he is recognized as a member of the underworld community.

There is probably no field of crime where loot is so readily presented for the taking as in the car theft business; and the chances of getting away with such thefts is considerably higher than in most other goods. Despite expert police communications and high-speed patrol cars which can be alerted within a few minutes of a car theft being discovered, the expert crooks know just when and where to operate. In the case of thieves specializing in spare parts, they need only half an hour to strip many of a car's components and remove them to a safe place. Small garages are the main distribution points for stolen parts and, as receivers, they are immensely difficult to detect in these days of mass-production when the identity of a wheel or some piece of machinery is lost once it is removed from its complete assembly.

Thieving is the commonest of crimes and, in some degree, almost every person is a thief two or three times a week. This is what students of human nature have come to realize in recent surveys of average behaviour in the world's larger cities and towns. Minor thieving and petty dishonesty among average people is a commonplace of modern living. It is reflected in the acceptance of privilege and graft in public and political life in the bigger communities of the world. The more highly organized life is, the more tolerant of dishonesty do we become until fiddling a few pounds off our income tax, leaving a bus or tram with our fare uncollected, or failing to pay a licence fee, is considered nothing more than a healthy individual revolt against the forms, laws, regulations and taxes with which modern life is beset.

The jump from such "human" behaviour to the behaviour of the real crook is, like madness, merely a matter of degree. The volume of shop-lifting, as any store-keeper knows, is staggering. Millions of pounds worth of small goods are stolen each year in a city like London or New York; in a recent estimate of shop-lifting losses in Sydney (population of less than two million) the annual figure was £500,000. This is the work of "amateurs", the people who take something for nothing on the spur of the moment and, in most cases, not because the stolen article is really needed but just because the impulse to steal is unpredictable and far commoner than is generally admitted. The tragedy occurs when a person does not know when to stop and suddenly becomes involved in the processes of the law.

The shock and shame of such discovery may produce widely differing reactions, varying from shame and contrition to resentment and revolt against conventional standards of behaviour. Among young people, the majority of recruits to the underworld are those who have been led into thinking crime is smart by established crooks. But many underworld beginners are driven to crime as an expression of hatred against the successful and established members of society they see about them.

An adolescent who, for one of a thousand reasons, may feel badly treated, unfairly handicapped or just lonely and miserable for want of affection, can easily turn to breaking the law as a compensation. The dangerous element in these situations is that there is a real excitement in "getting away with something" that is forbidden. Thieves are never bored when they are stealing, and there is, to them, a real sense of achievement in carrying out a robbery successfully. They pit their wits and risk their reputations in a gamble with authority and, when it pays off, they are greatly stimulated. Unfortunately such beginnings in crime are rarely detected for the offences are slight and, as the beginners have no reason to be suspected, they operate with almost complete freedom.

A successful businessman once confessed that at the age of fourteen he was a practised shoplifter. All his family Christmas presents that year were stolen from department stores. "Then," he said, "I broke into a soft drink factory one Sunday afternoon and stole a crate of lemonade. It was an exhilarating adventure. I can still remember the thrill of getting away unnoticed. After that came the theft of a woman's handbag from a neighbouring house.

"There were several rings in it and I tore out the stones and took the gold to a jeweller. I explained the rings were my mother's and that she was too ashamed to bring them in herself for sale as old gold. The story went across without a hitch and I felt a sudden sense of power, a contempt for honest men. If people were as easy to fool as this, why not make a career of thieving?

"It was exciting to plan an operation and the execution of a job was by far the most thrilling experience I had enjoyed. But I stopped my career as a sneak-thief as suddenly as I had begun it. I gave it up for reading. Just like that. My new passion led me to the temptation of stealing books from libraries and shops, but for some reason I could not fathom at the time this seemed a despicable thing to do.

"I realize now that had I been caught at my thieving I could have easily become a professional thief. But I was lucky. I was not caught and I stopped in time."

"I stopped in time." In those four words lie the difference between a life in the underworld and a life as a normal, honest person. The businessman was one of the lucky ones. Perhaps it was not luck, but his superior intelligence which led him away from crime.

There are a thousand and one forms of theft and as many reasons why people become criminals. Given the opportunity, most of us succumb to the temptation of getting something for nothing. Every society is made up of human individuals and, as long as that is the case, every society will have its share of crime. What is disturbing, in our time, is that the share of crime in our lives has grown so large.